Pretty Flowers

Coloring Book for Adults

Avri Maplewood

Published by Renuti™

THIS BOOK BELONGS TO

TABLE OF CONTENTS (1 OF 2)

Petunias	9
Mandevillas	11
Lupines	13
Forget Me Nots	15
Cosmos	17
Carnations	19
Canna Lilies	21
Asters	23
Columbine Flowers	25
Dianthus	27
Orienpet Lilies	29
Roses of Sharon	31
Dahlias	33
Daisies	35
Desert Roses	37
Chrysanthemums	39
Amaryllises	41
Bird of Paradise Flowers	43
Polyanthuses	45
Red Ginger Flowers	47
Nasturtiums	49
Clematis	51
Anemones	53
Calendulas	55
Daffodils	57

<u>TABLE OF CONTENTS (2 OF 2)</u>

Blue Water Lilies	59
Sweet Peas	61
Tea Roses	63
Pelargoniums	65
Butterfly Pea Flowers	67
Christmas Roses (Hellebores)	69
Hollyhocks	71
Canterbury Bells Flowers	73
Heleniums	75
Penstemons	77
Straw Flowers	79
Crocosmias	81
Delphiniums	83
Hyacinths	85
Oriental Lilies	87
Ranunculus	89
Heliconias	91
Gerberas	93
King Proteas	95
Lisianthuses	97
Cannonball Flowers	99
Cockscomb Flowers	101
Bearded Irises	103
Wisteria	105
Oleanders	107

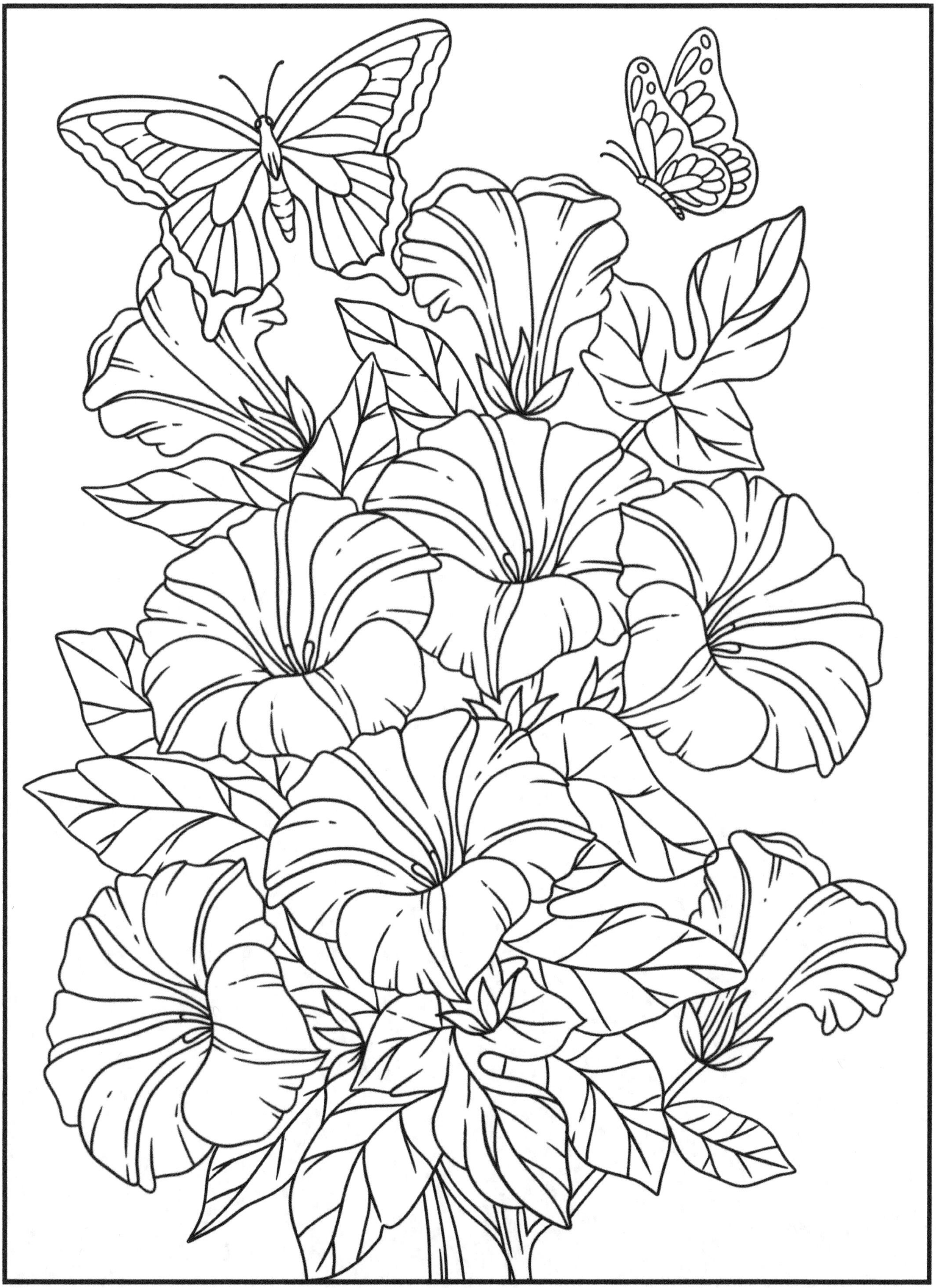

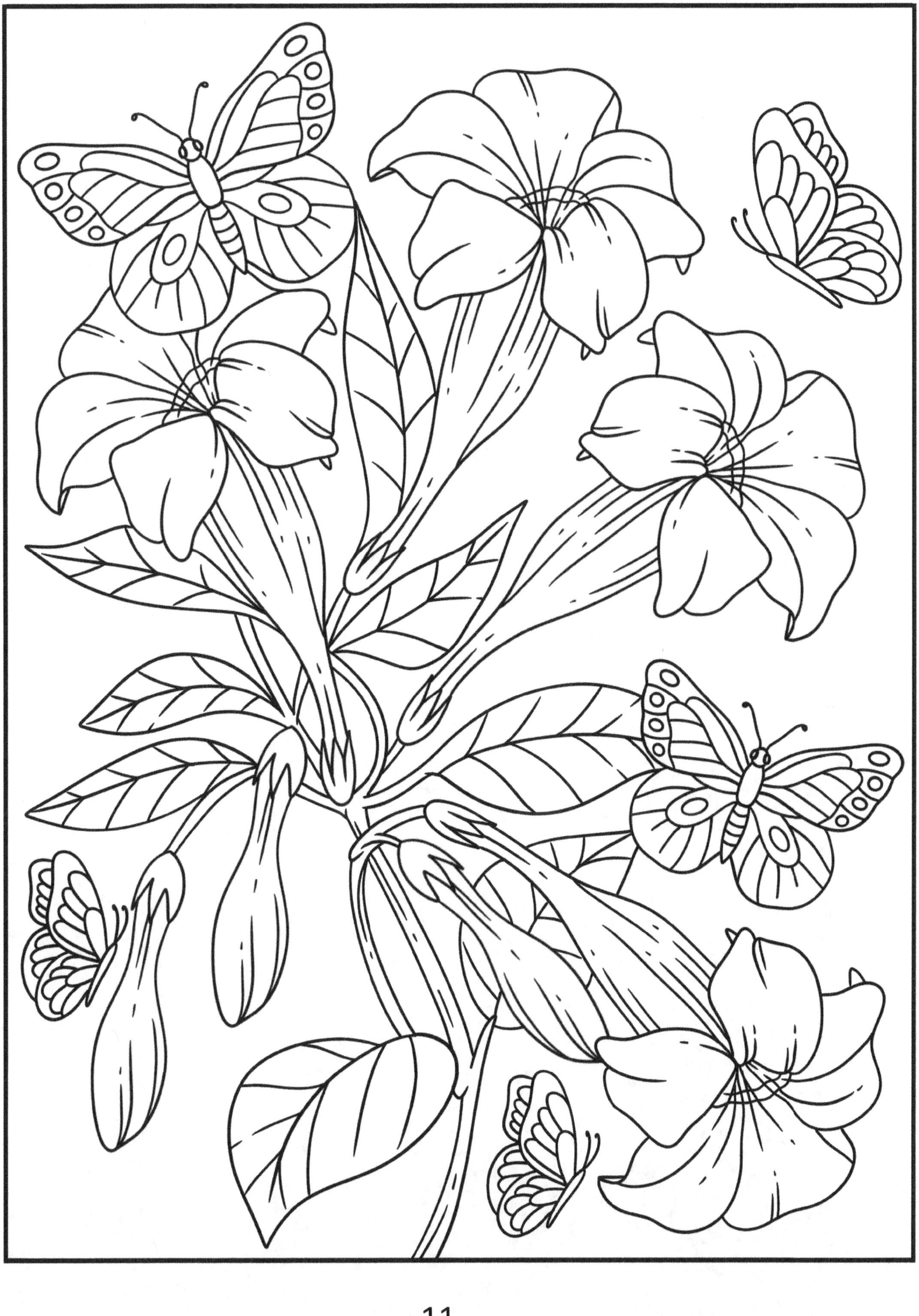

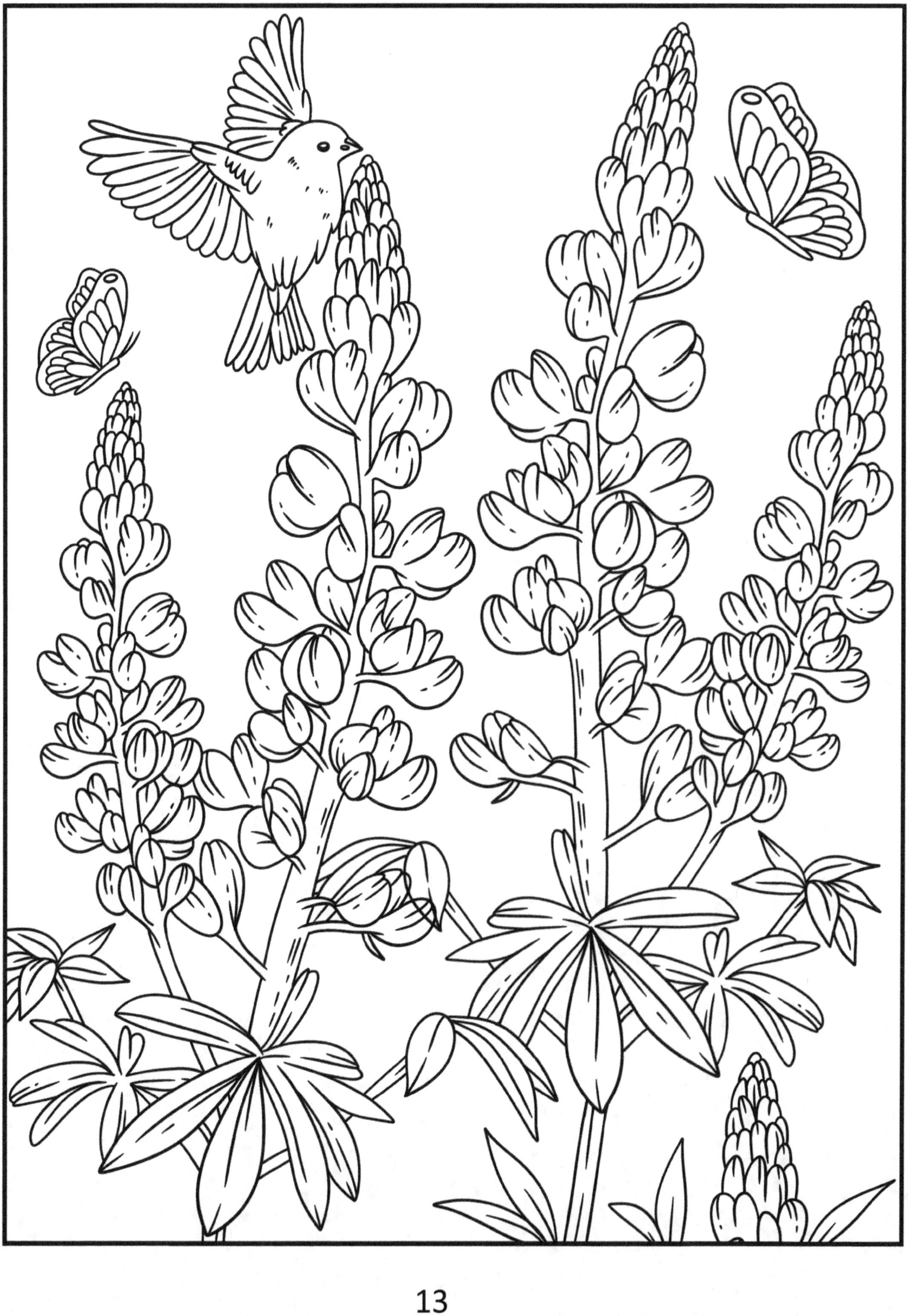

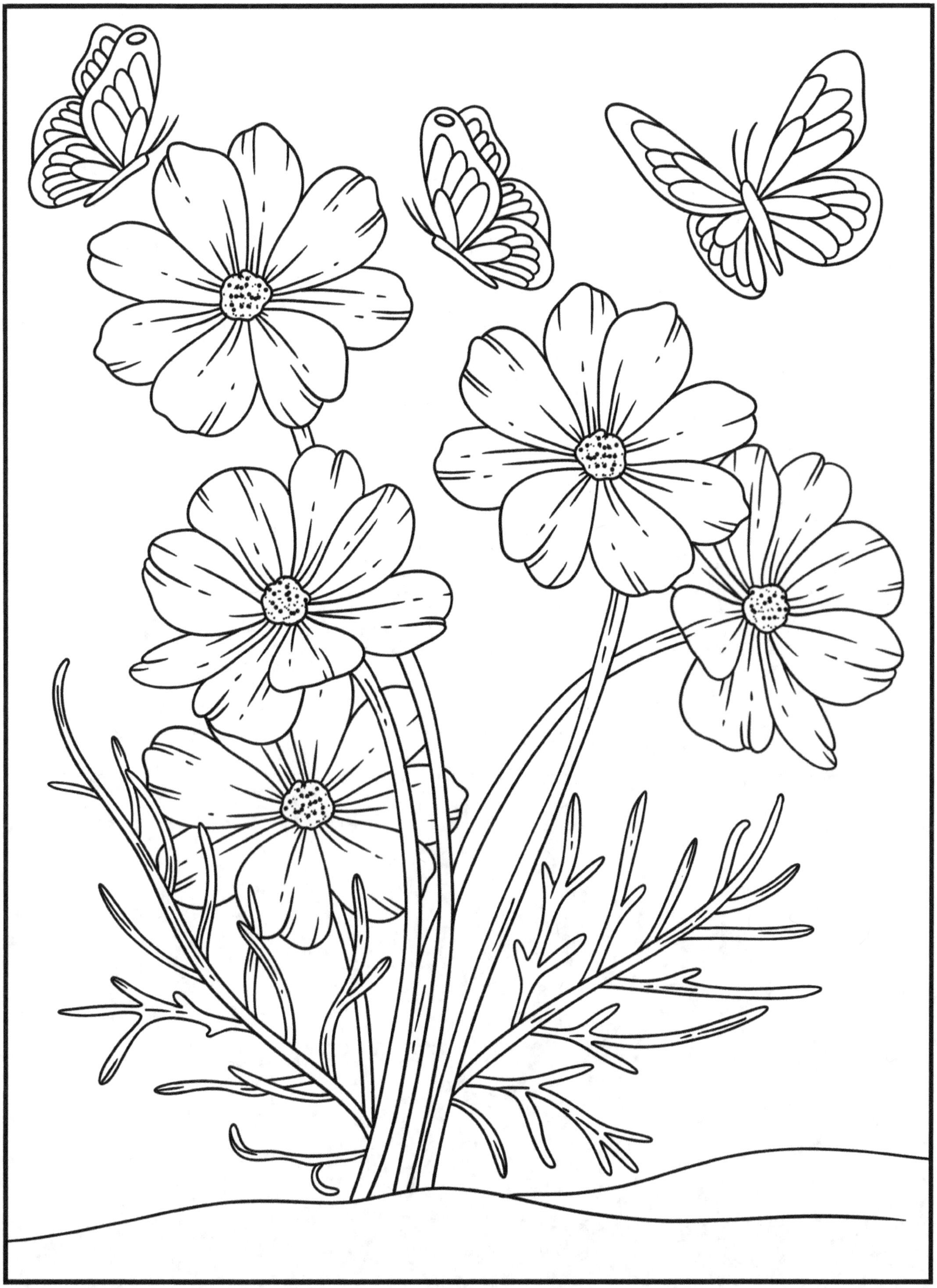

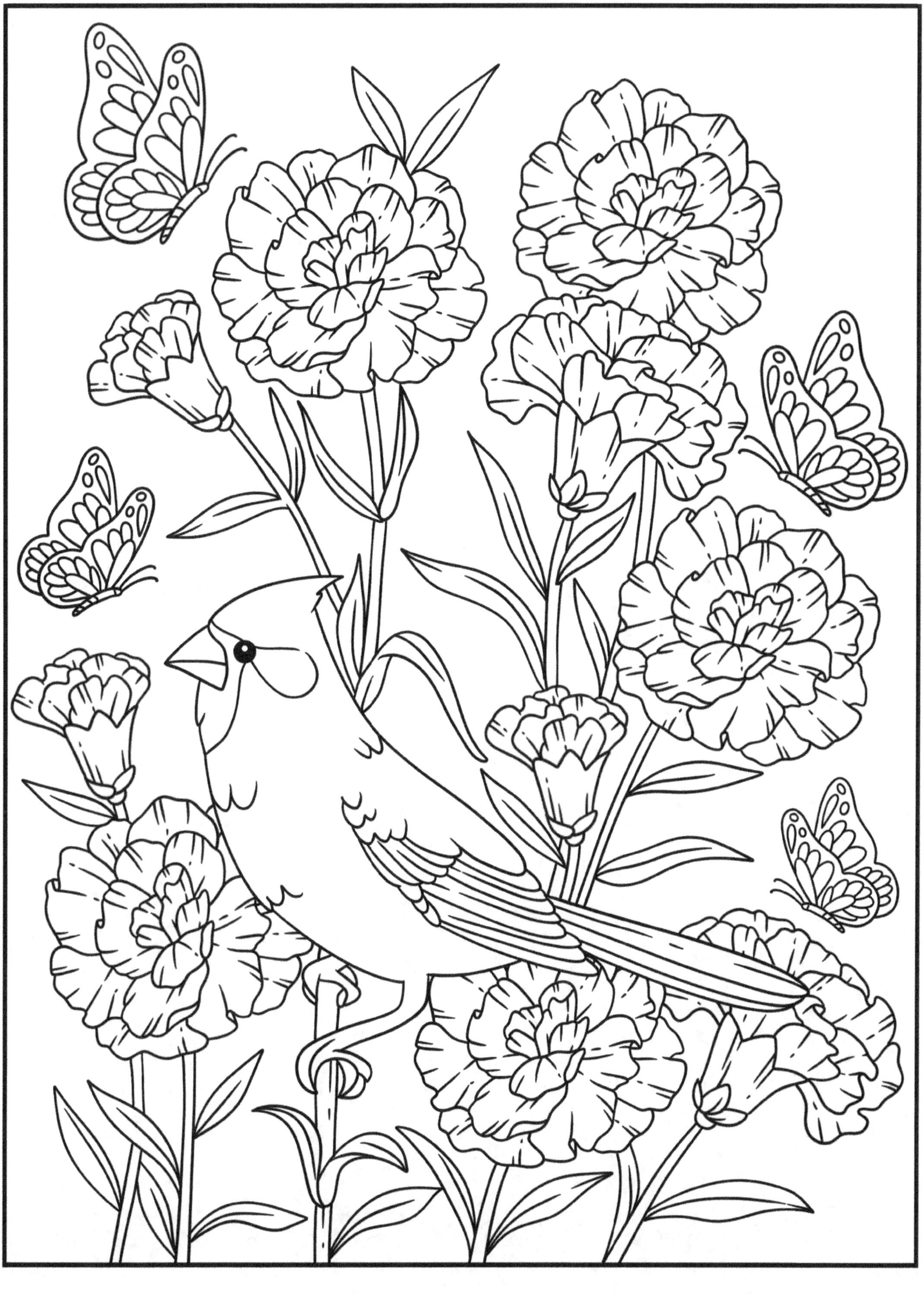

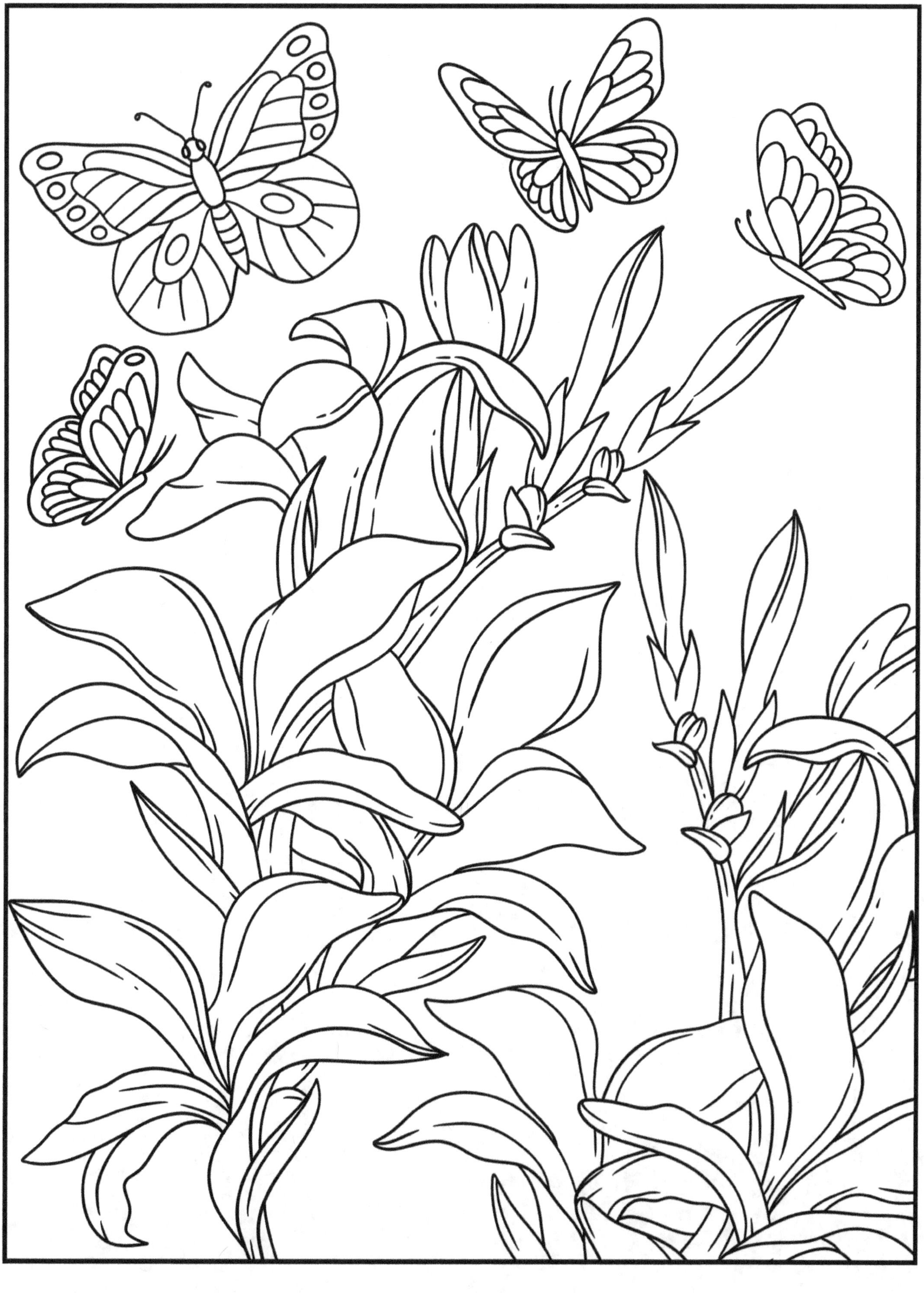

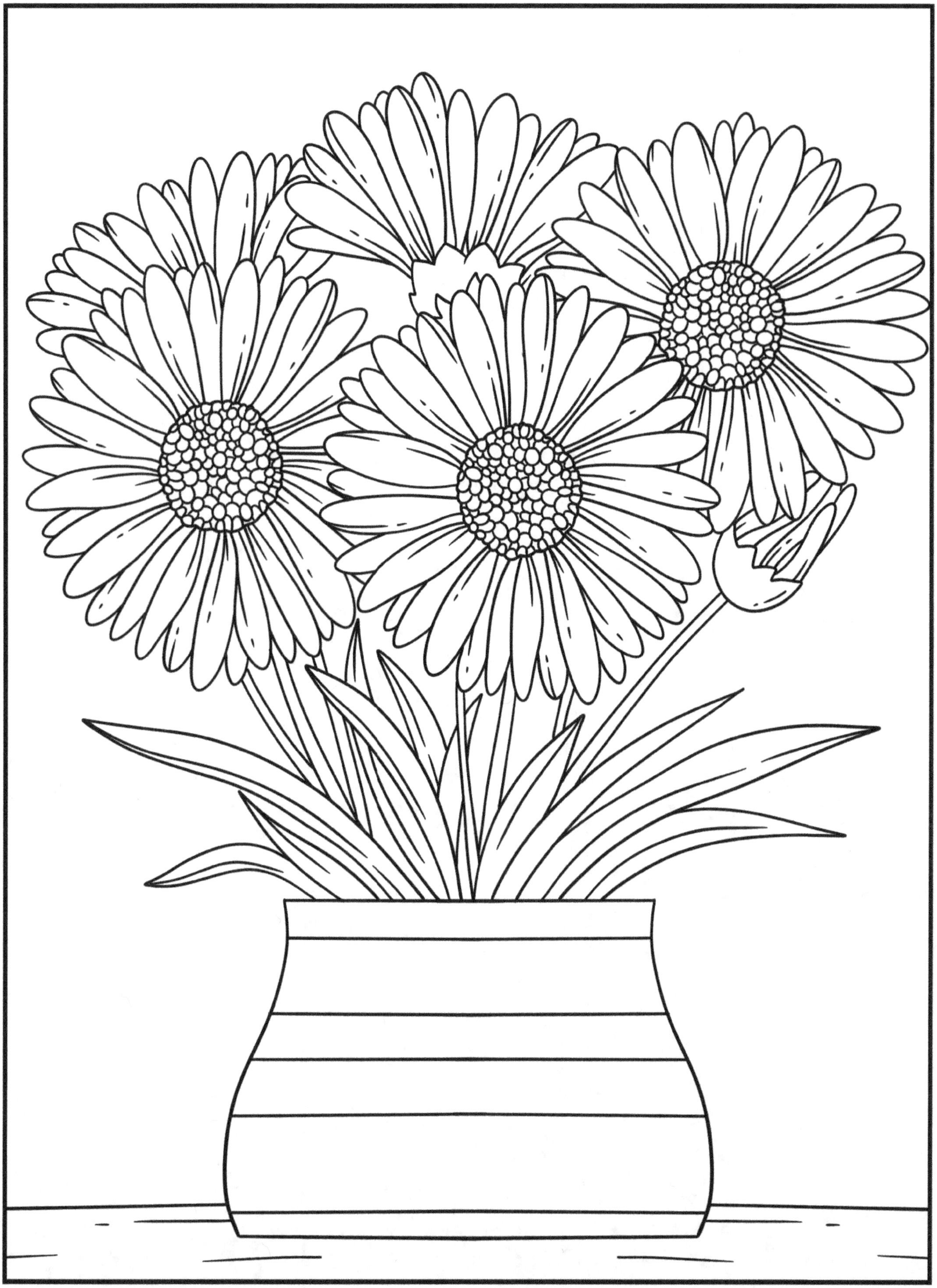

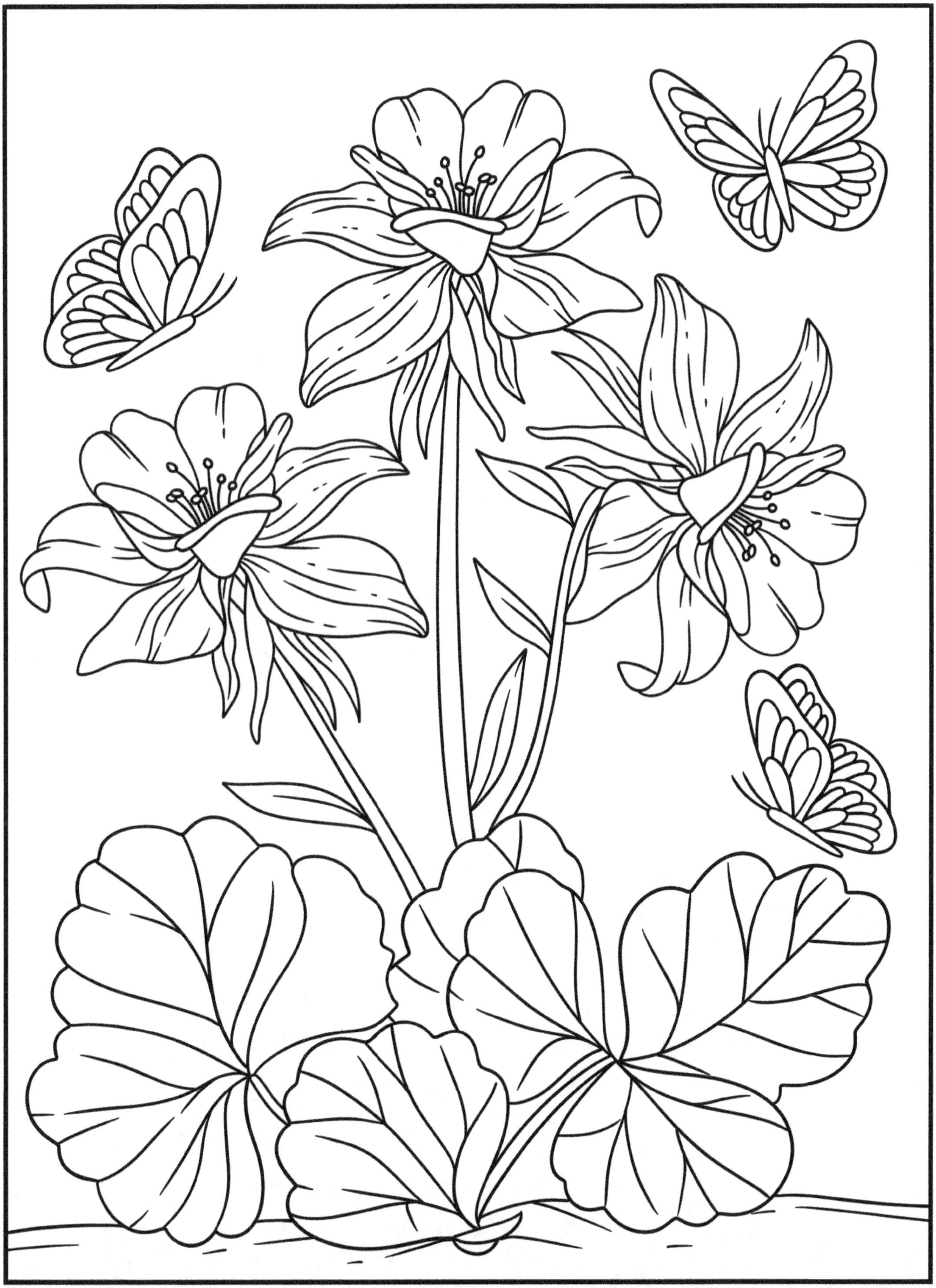

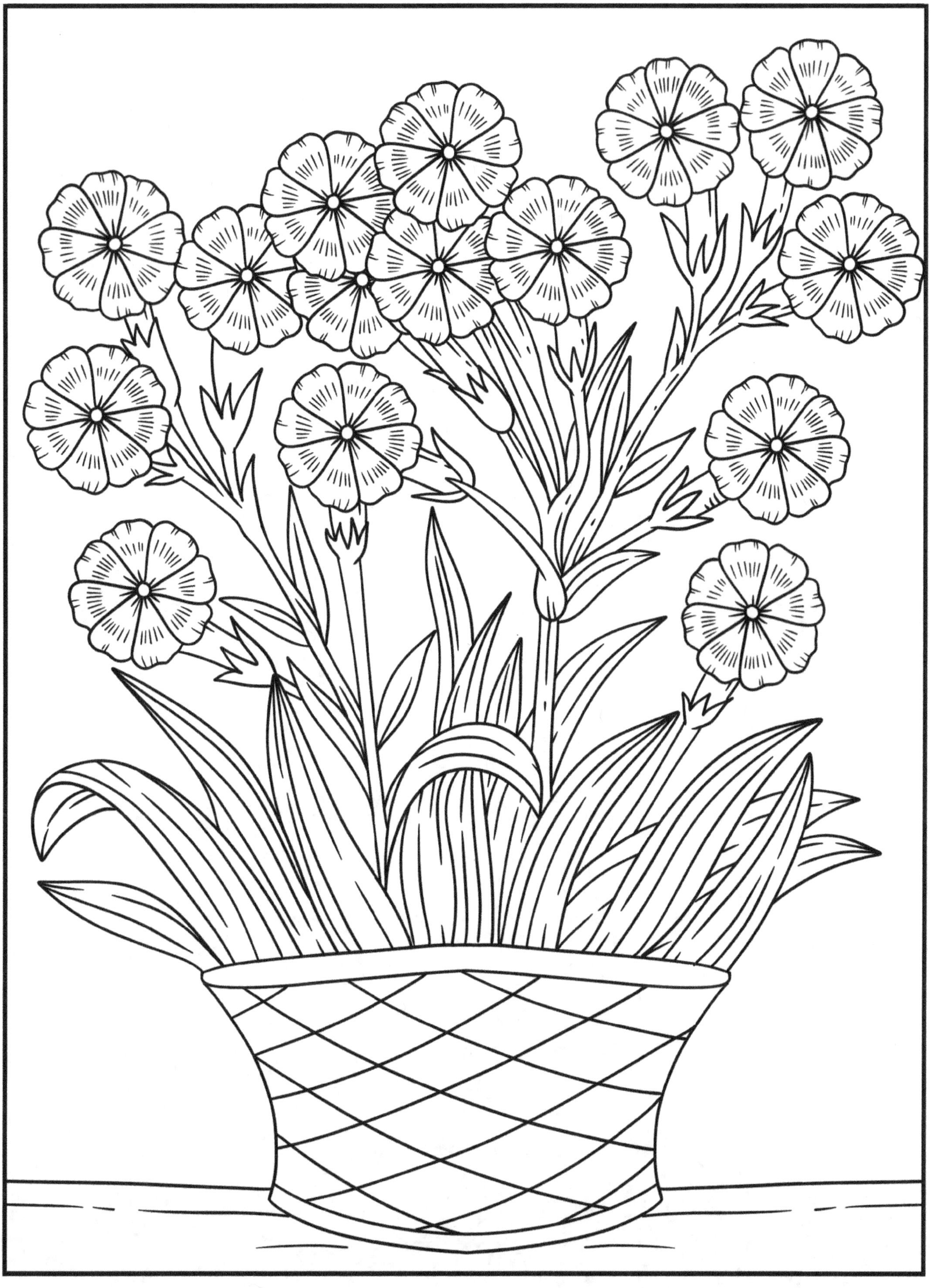

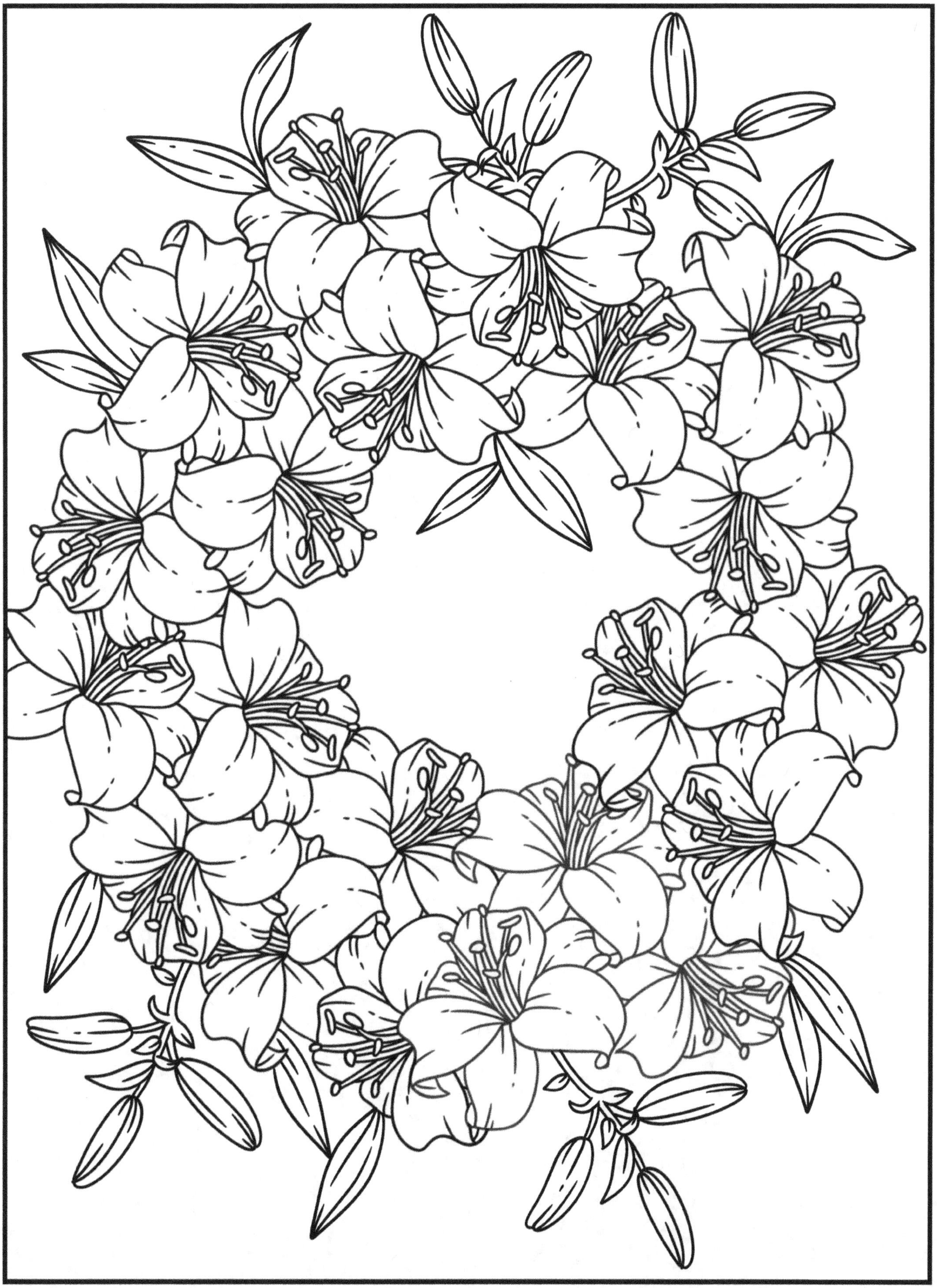

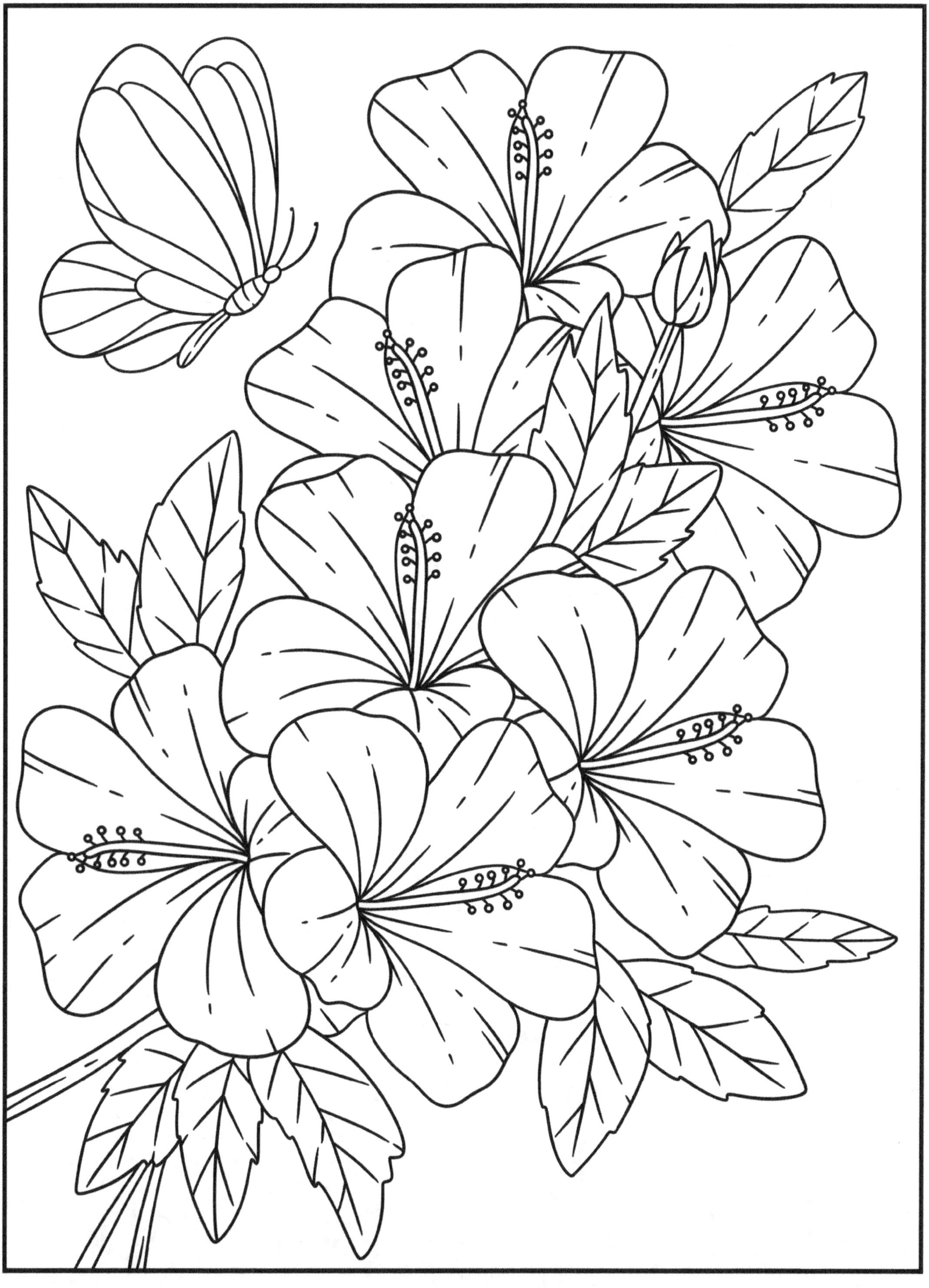

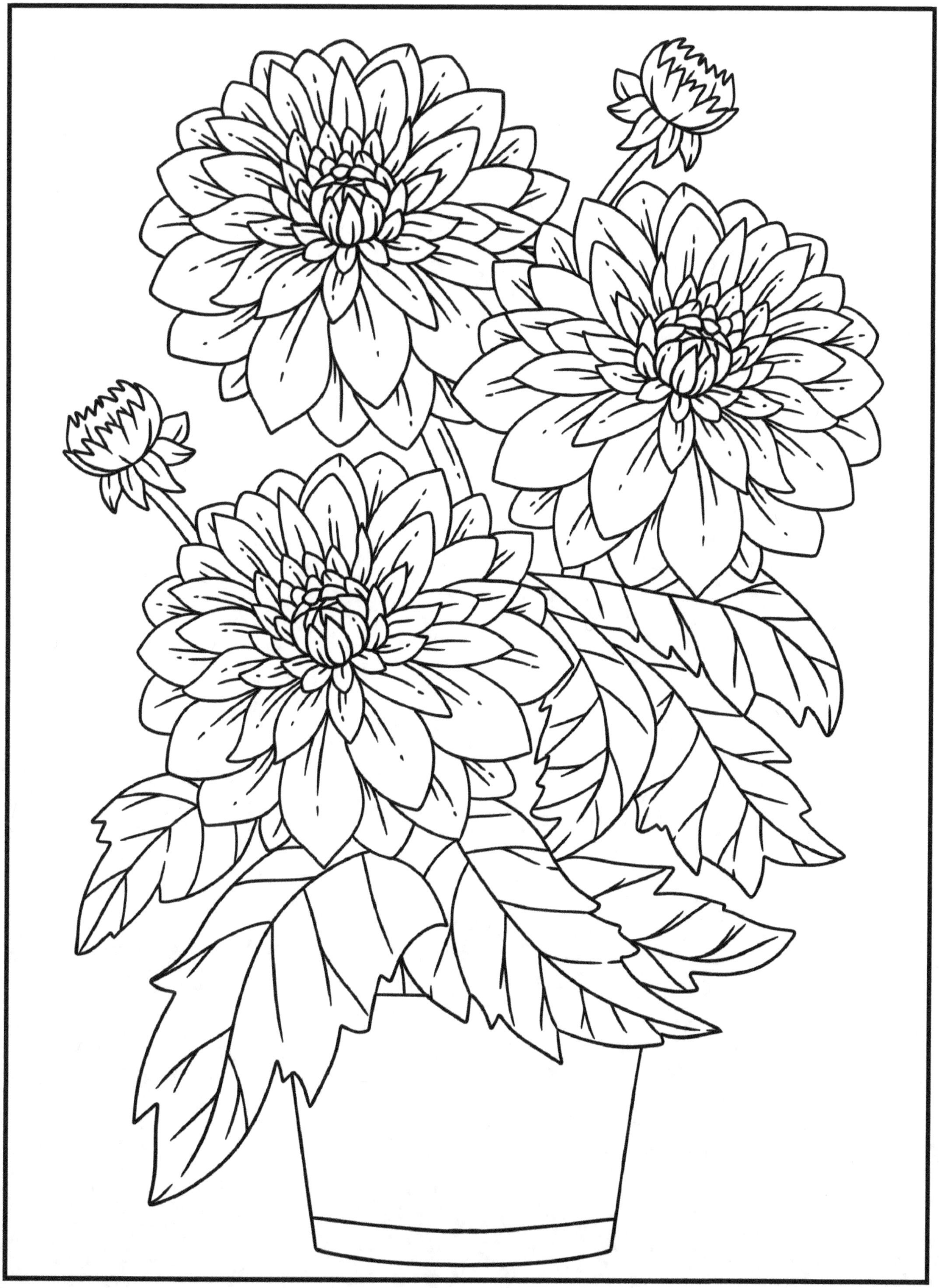

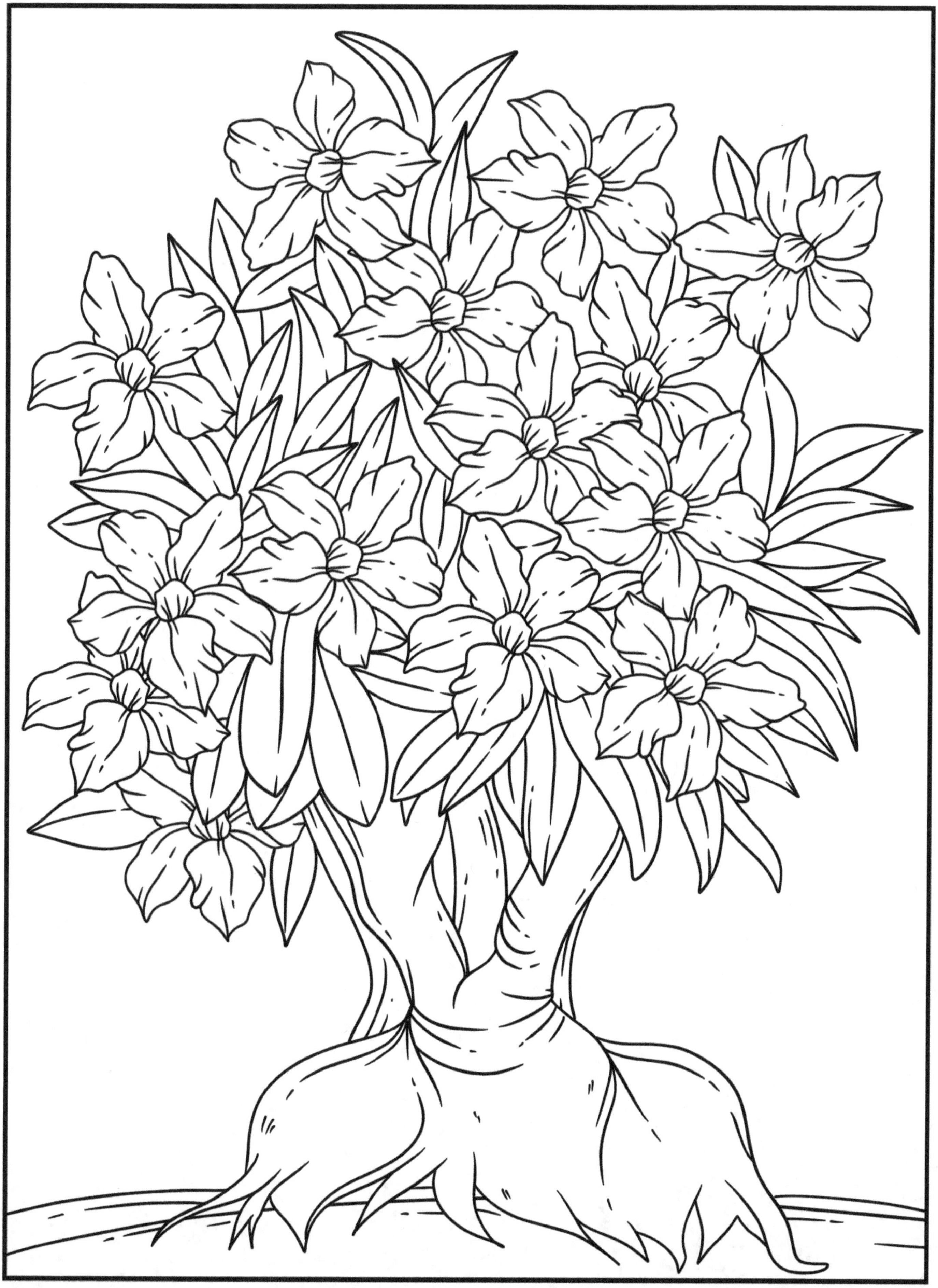

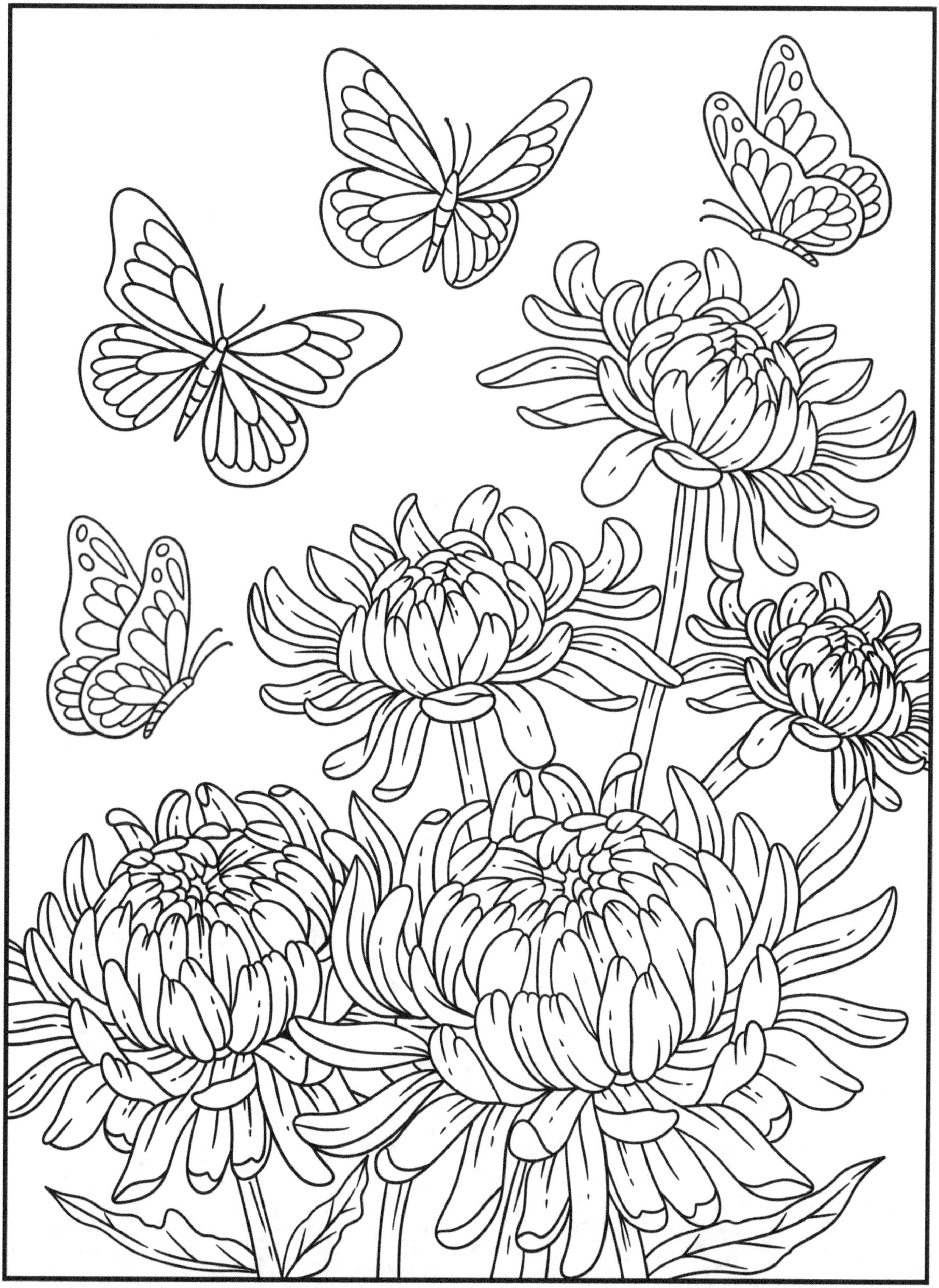

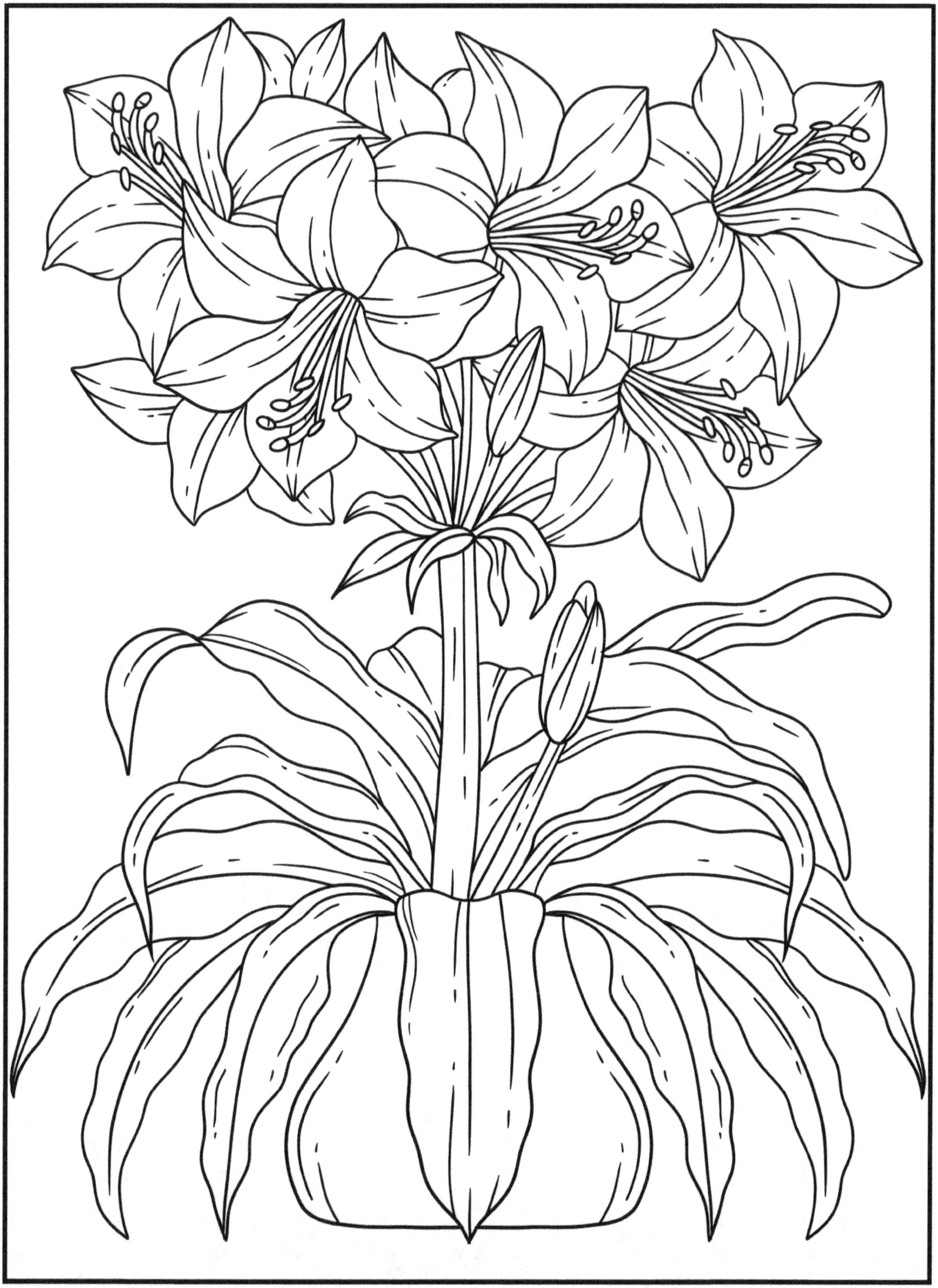

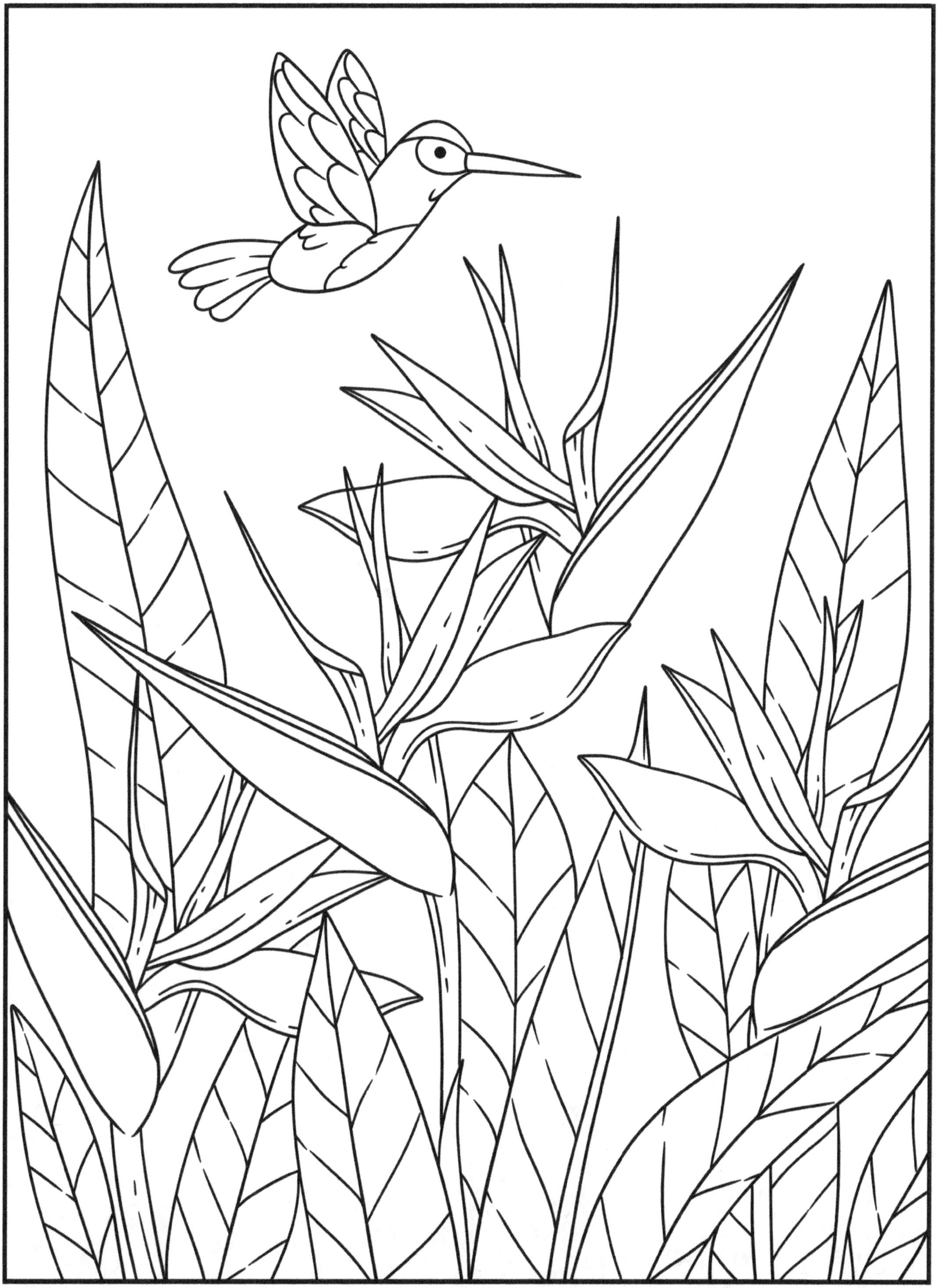

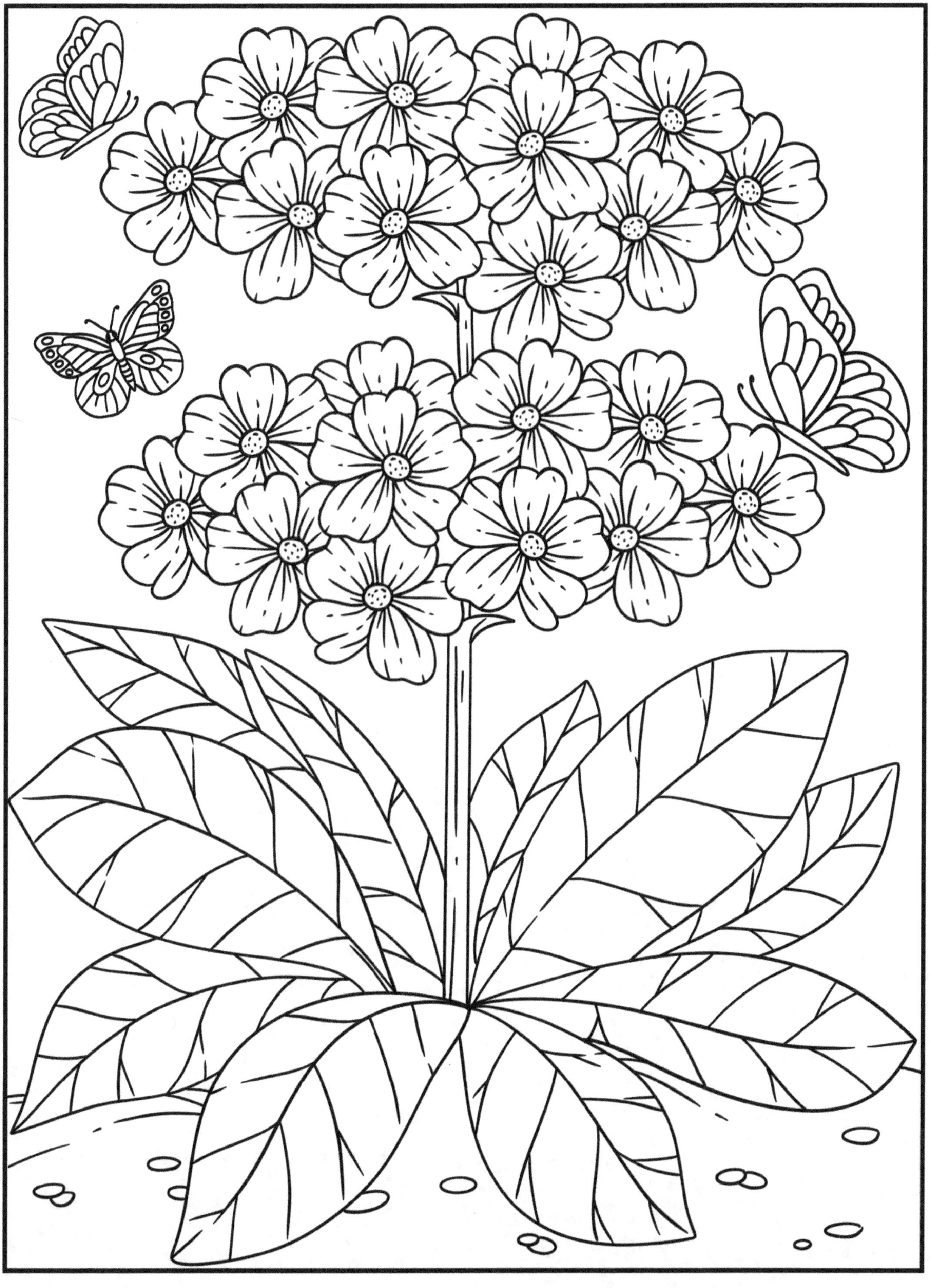

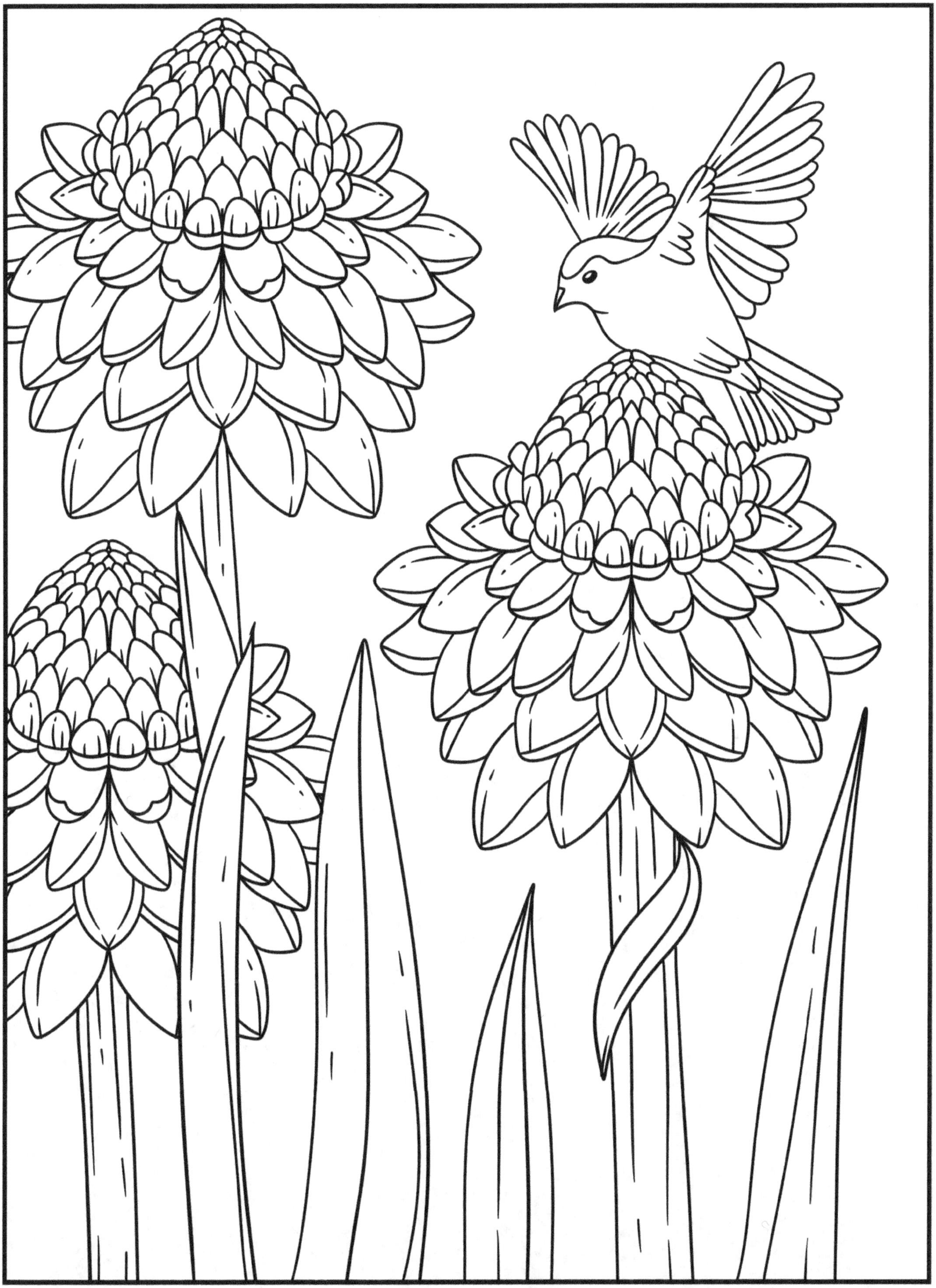

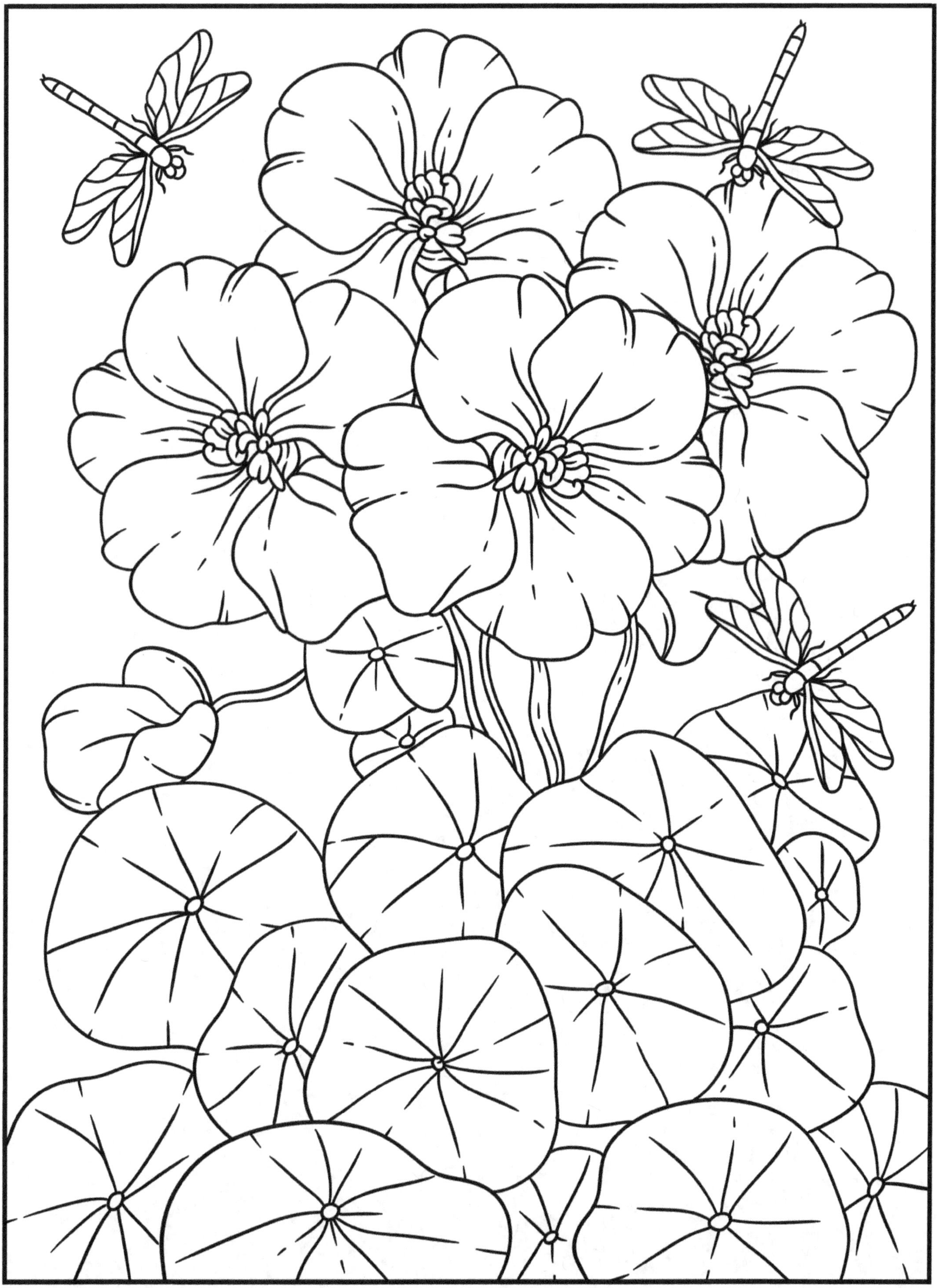

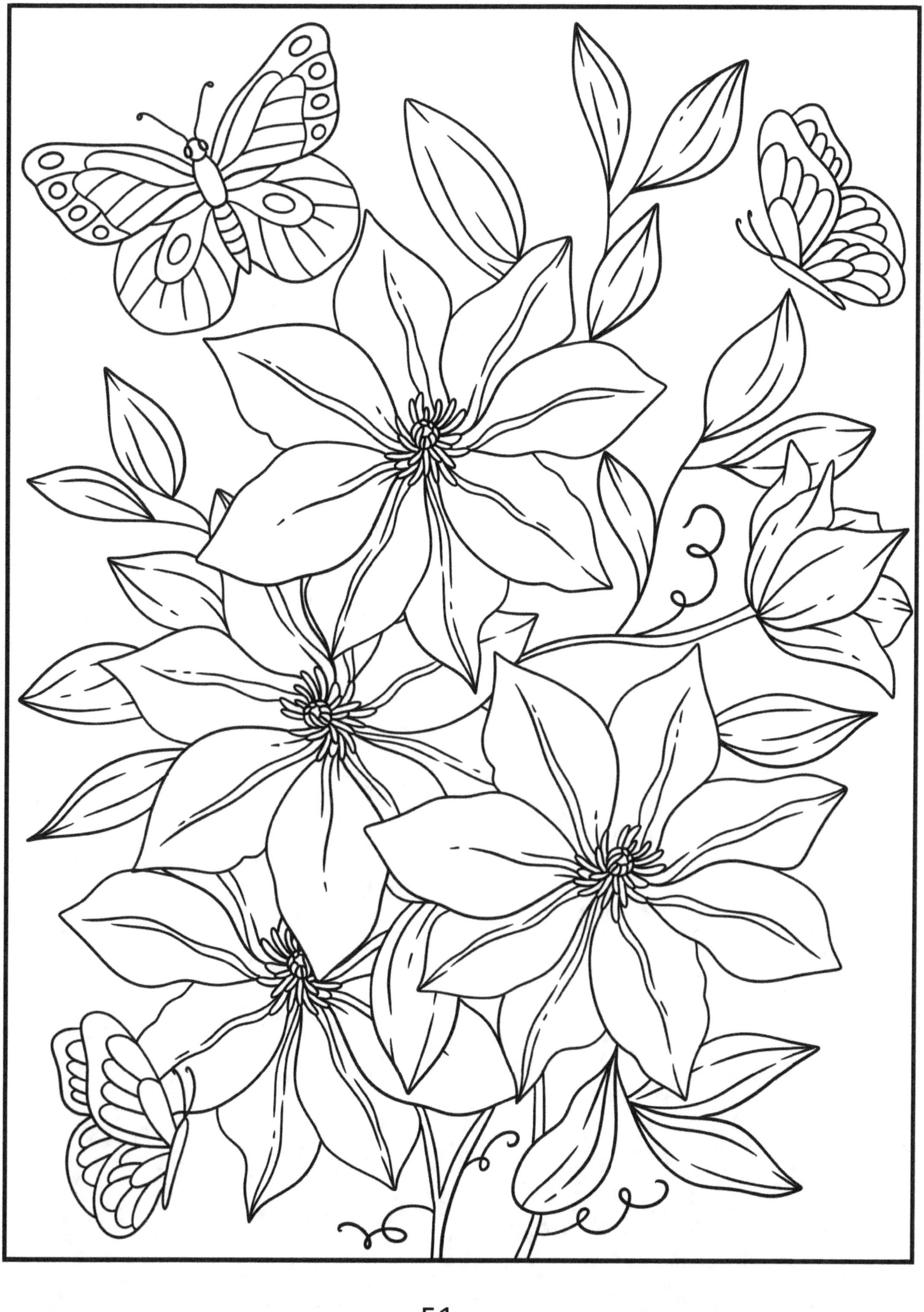

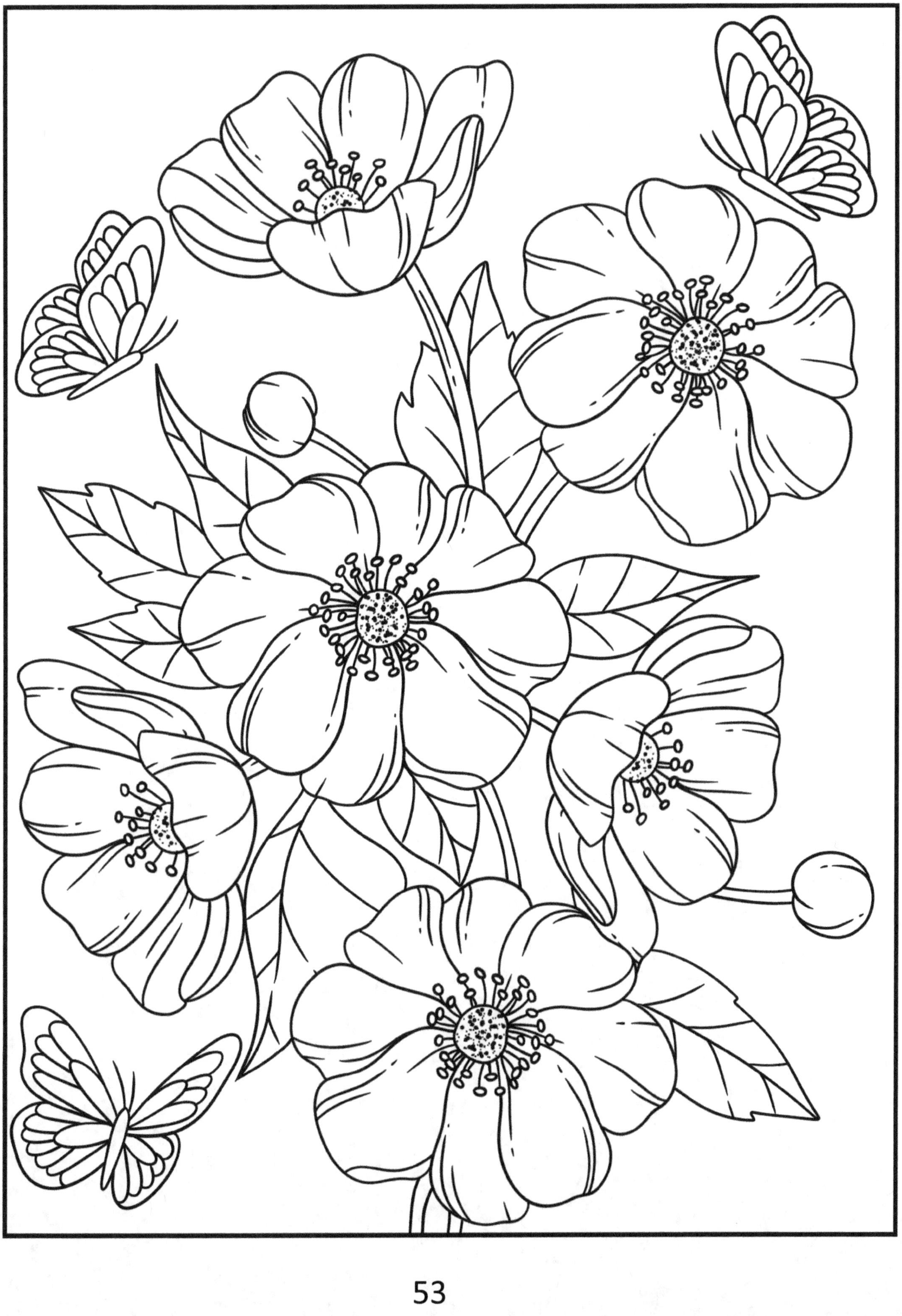

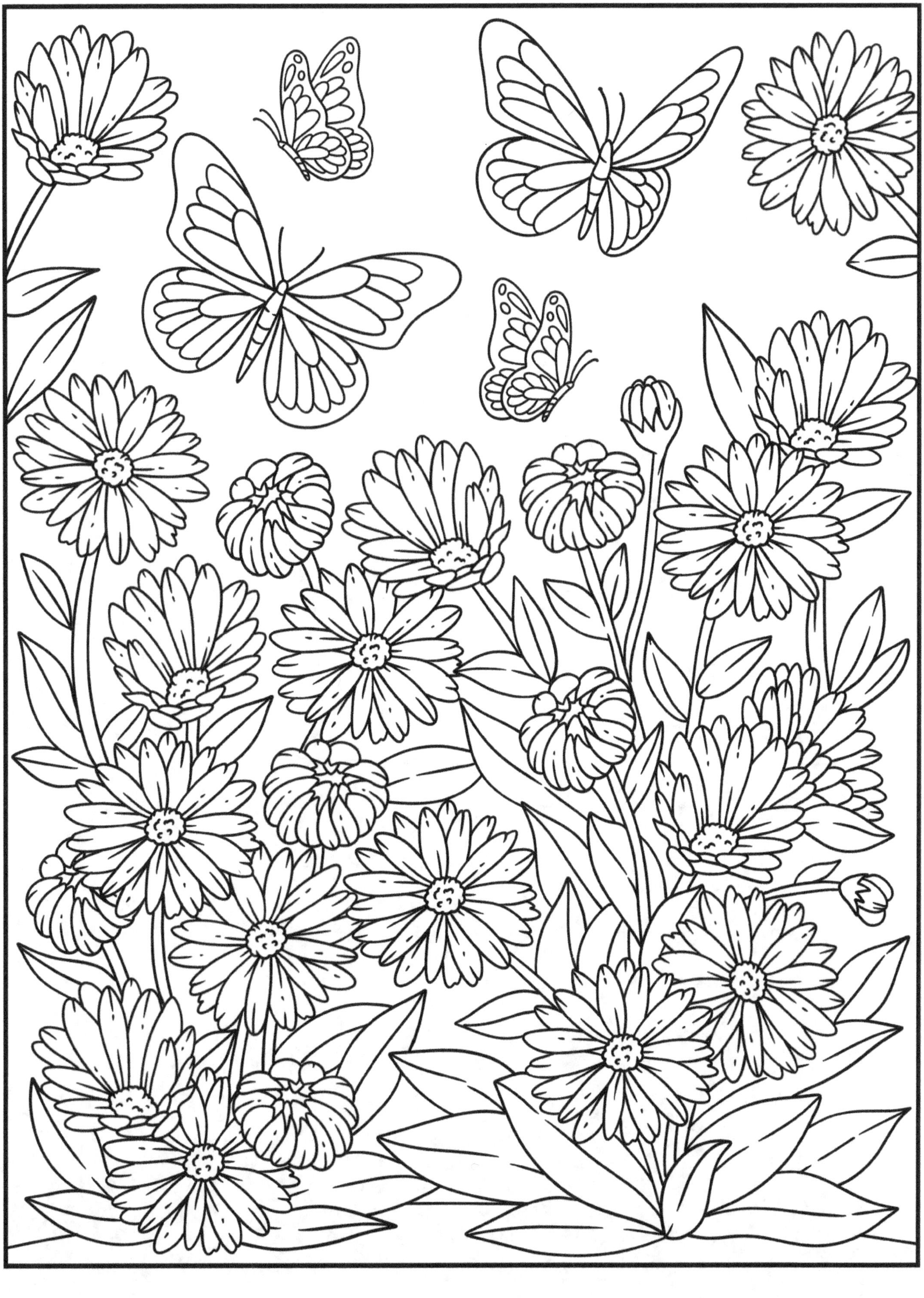

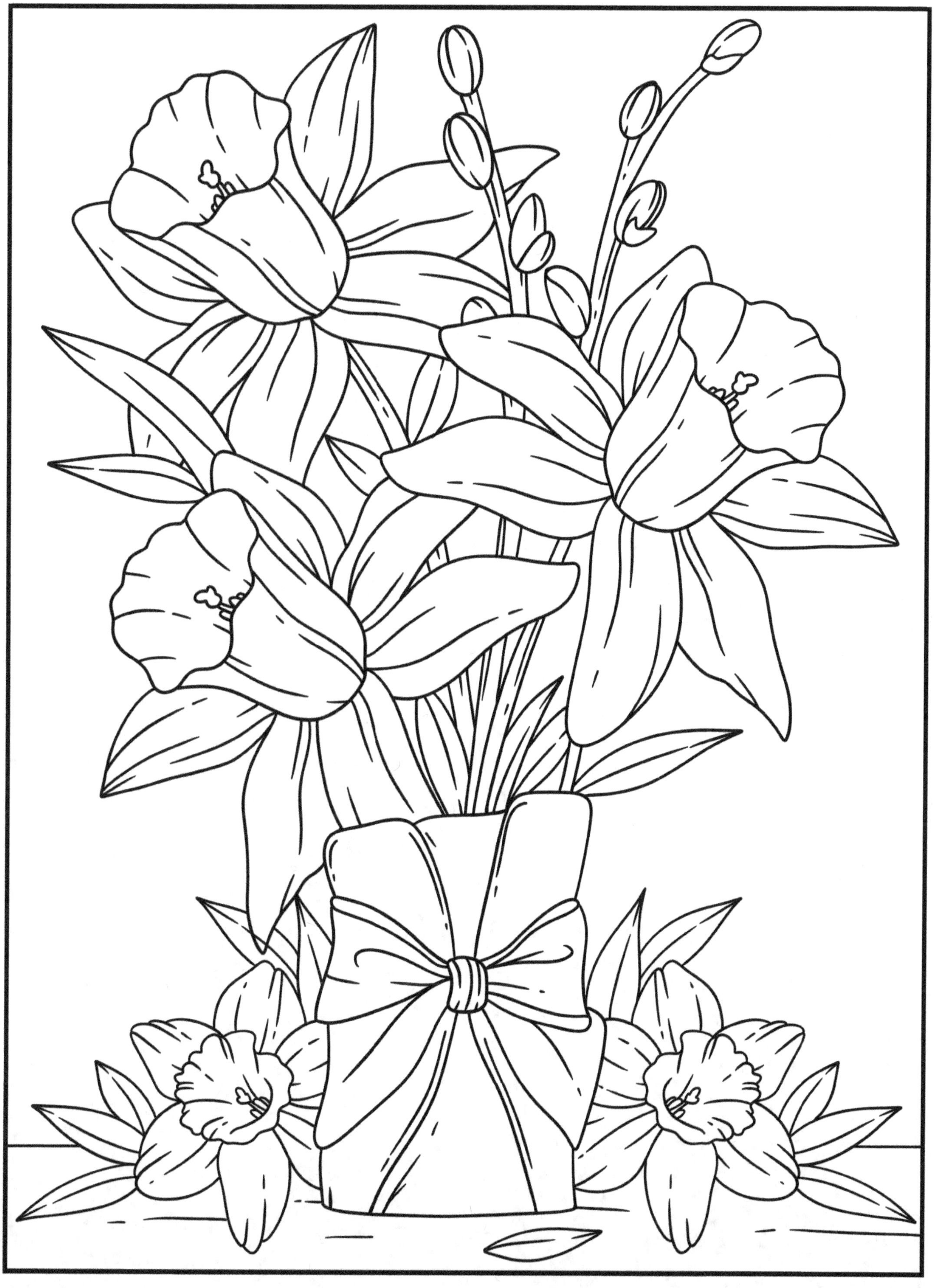

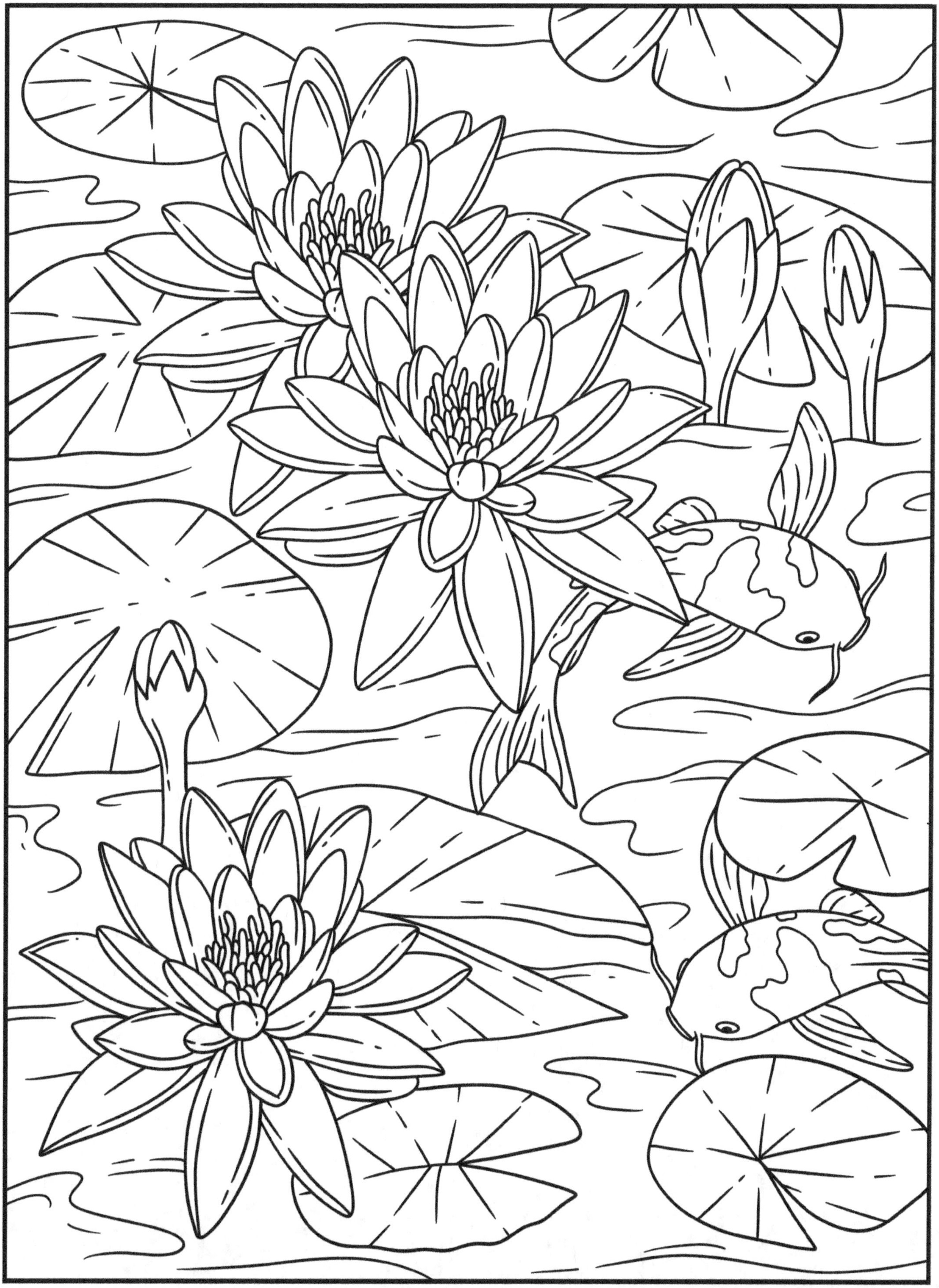

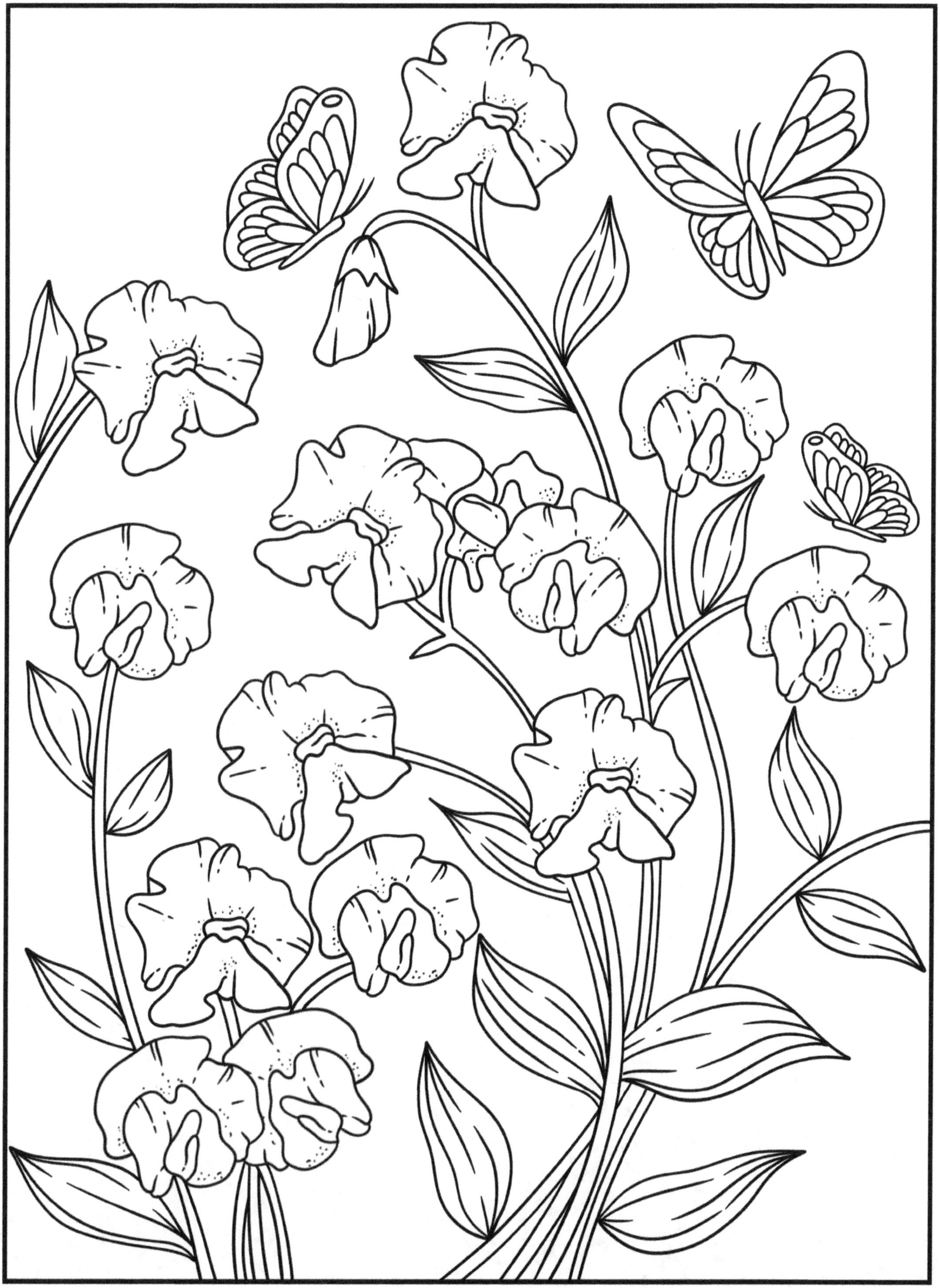

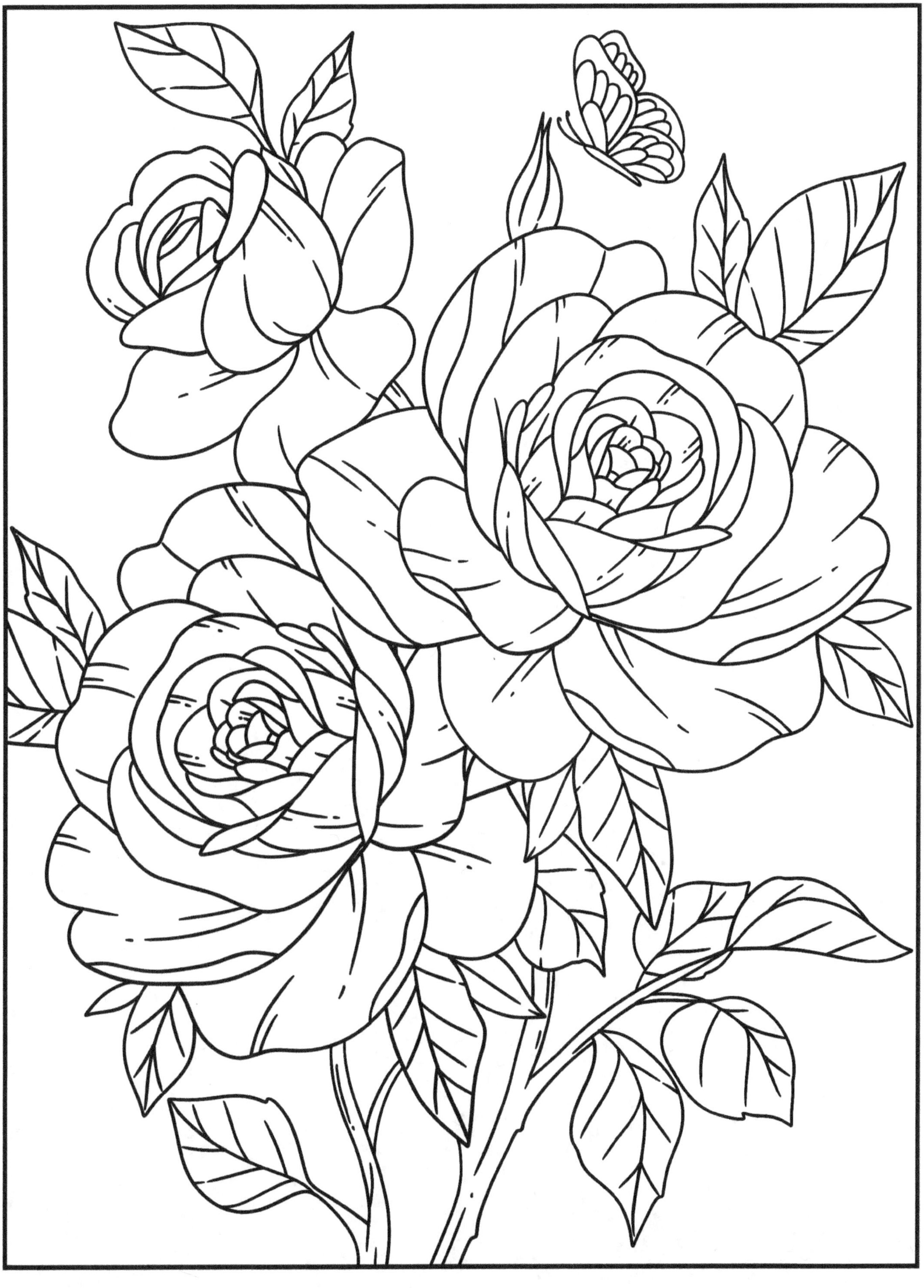

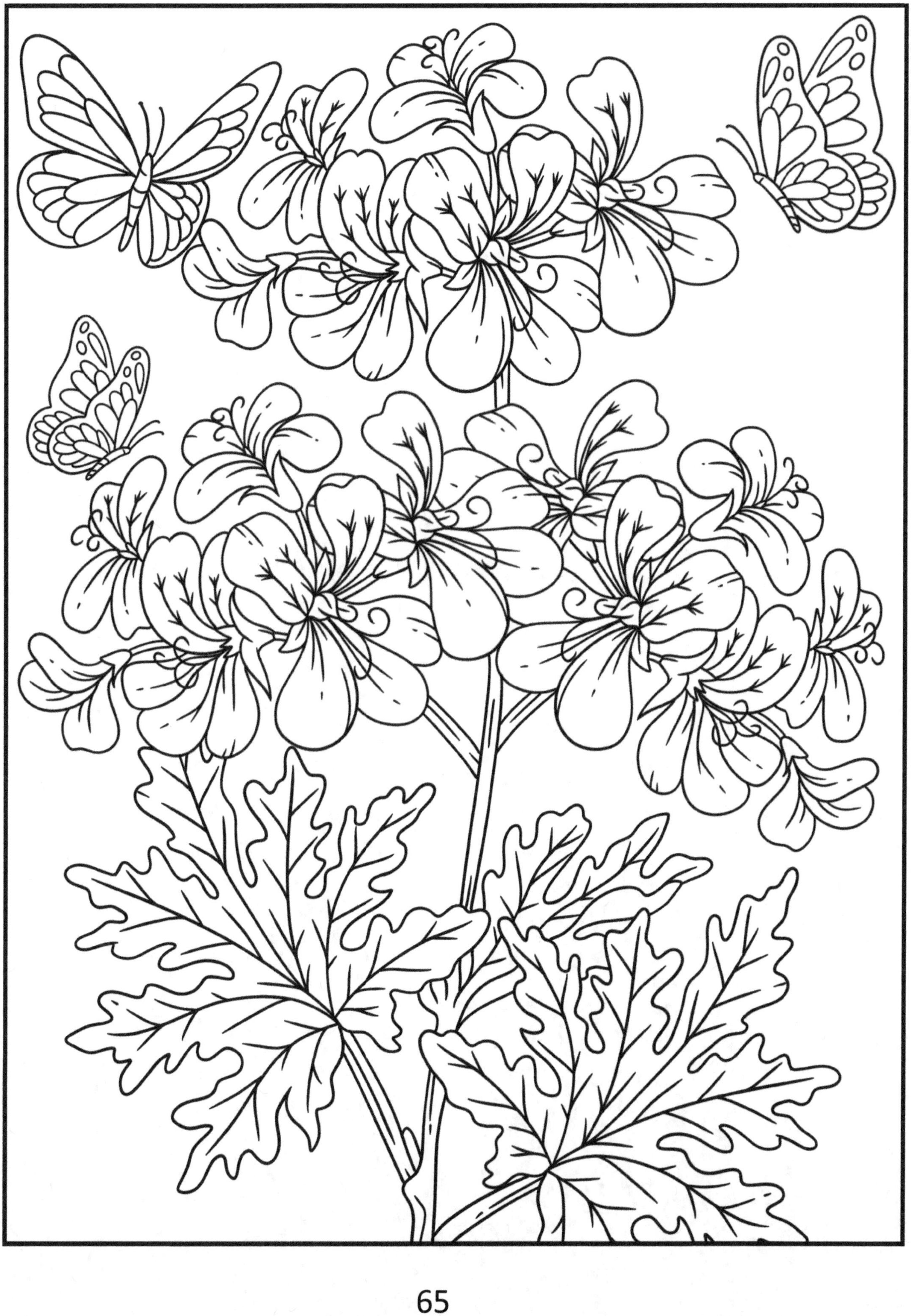

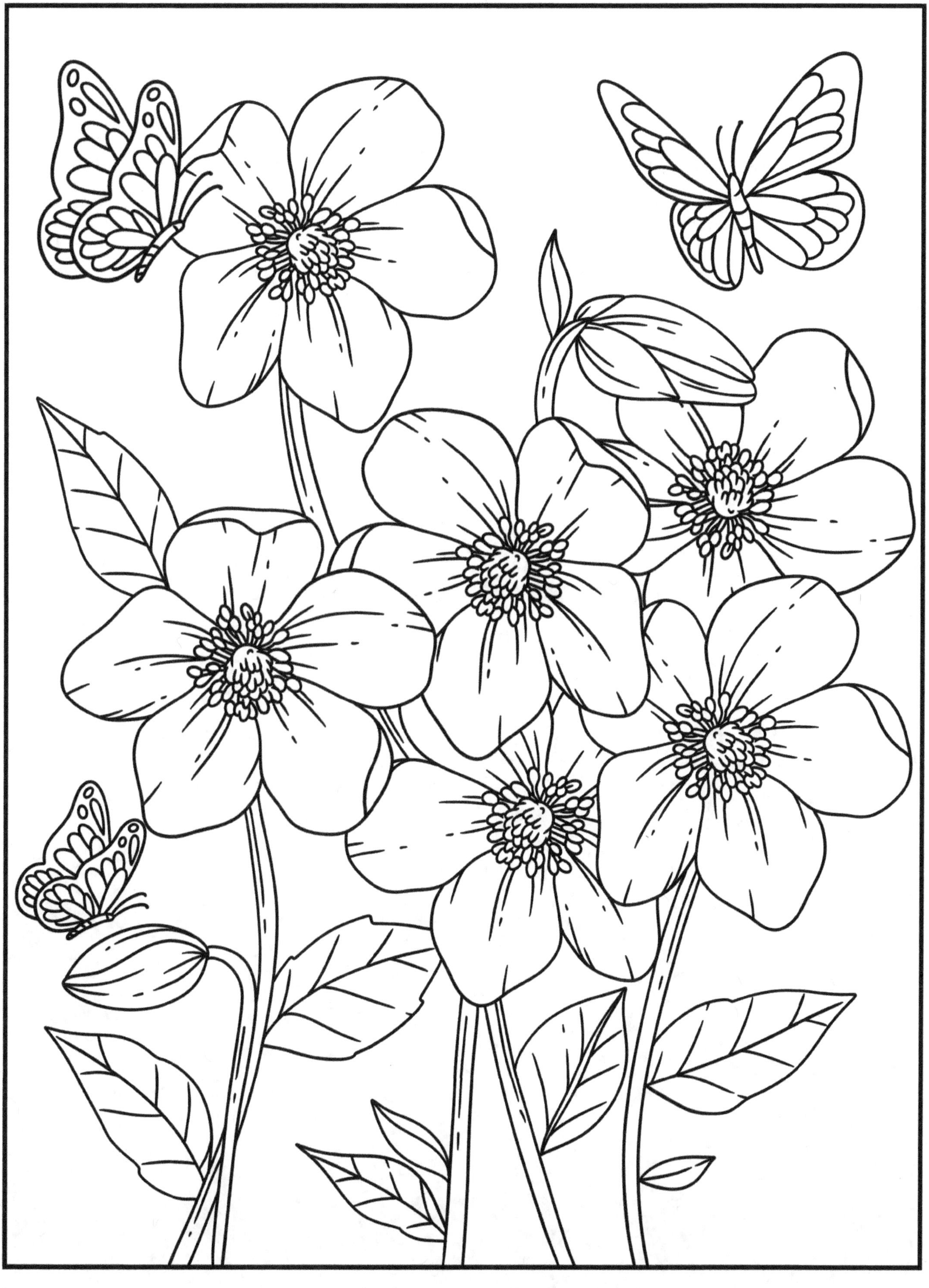

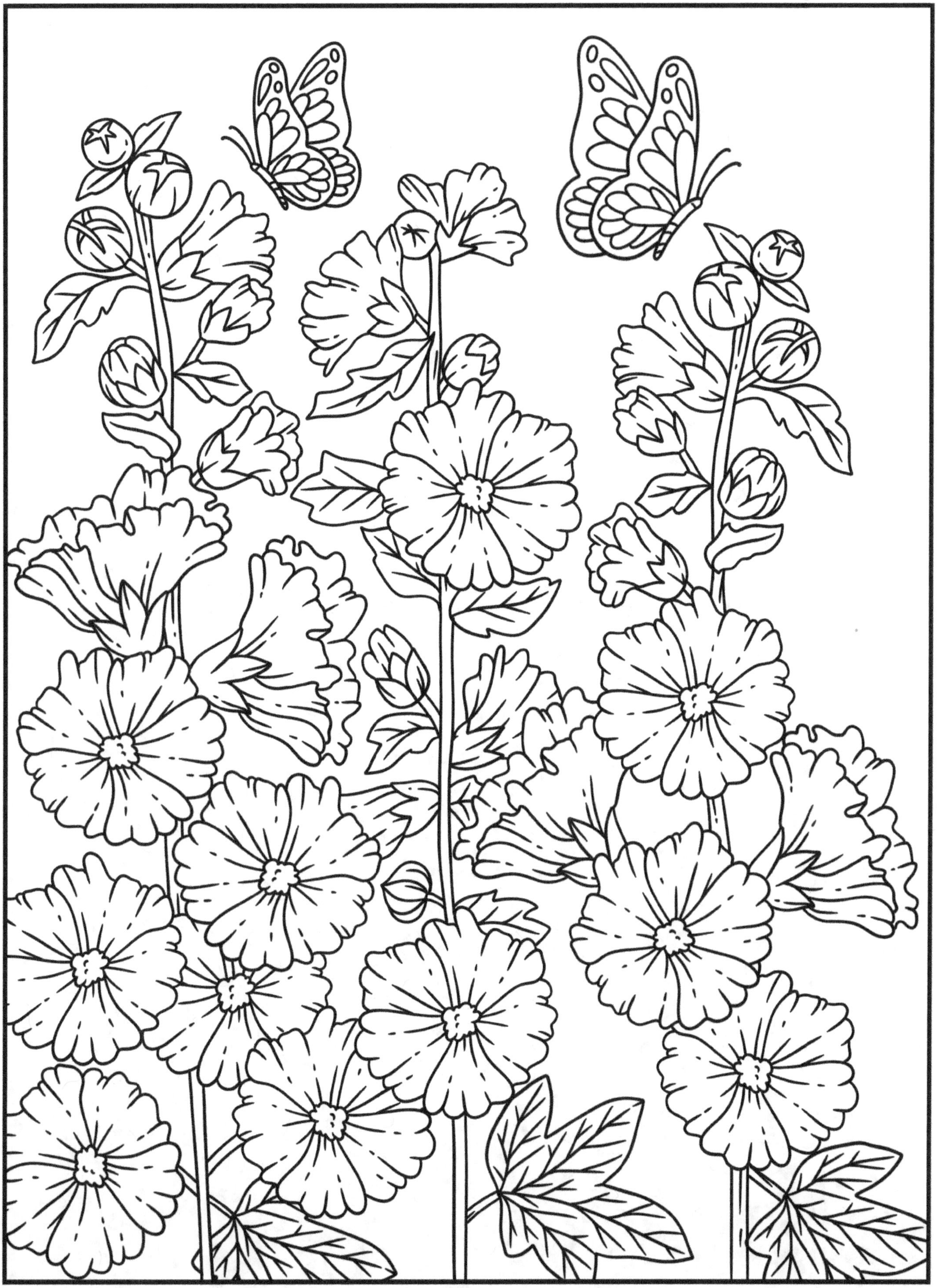

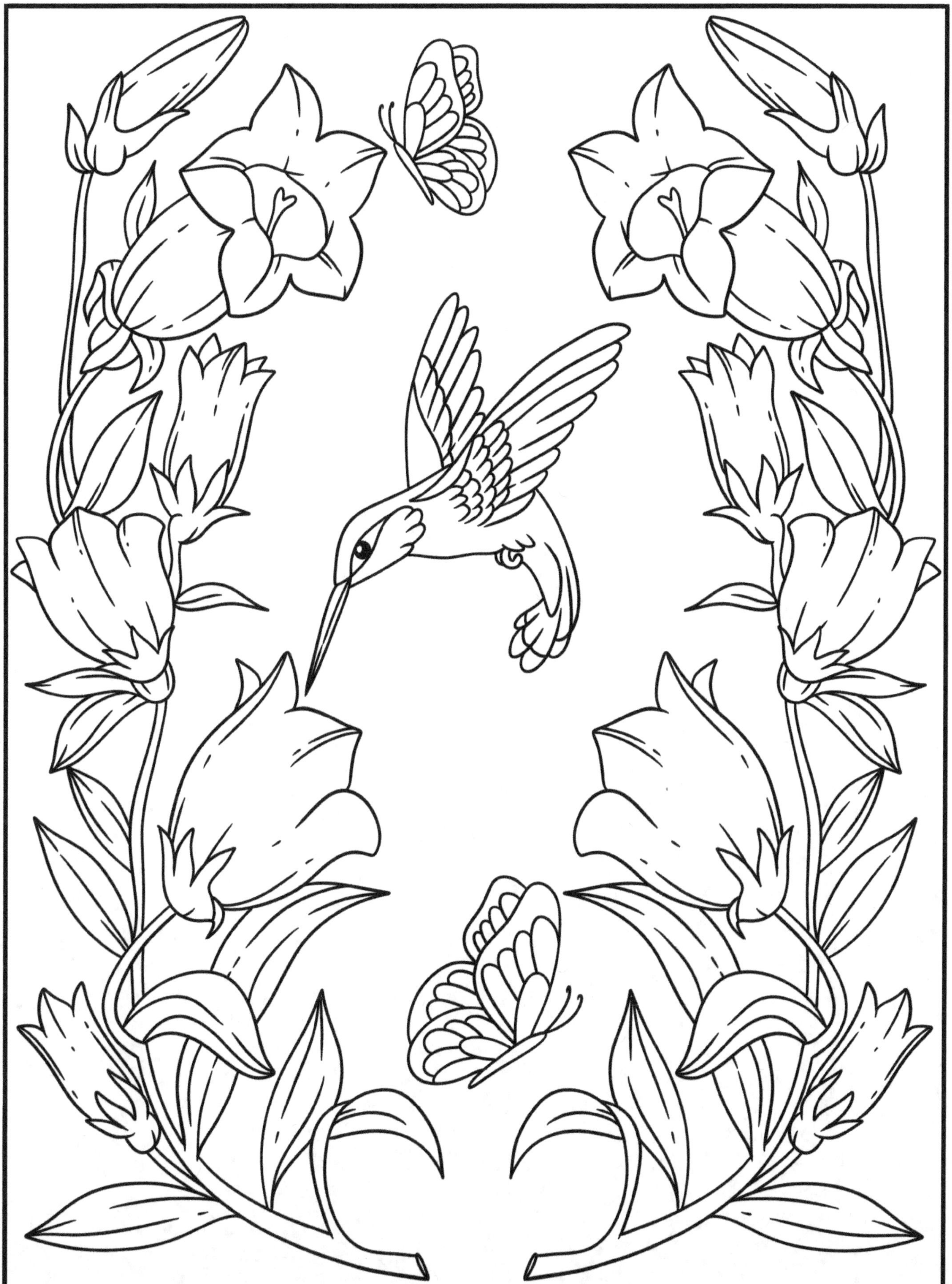

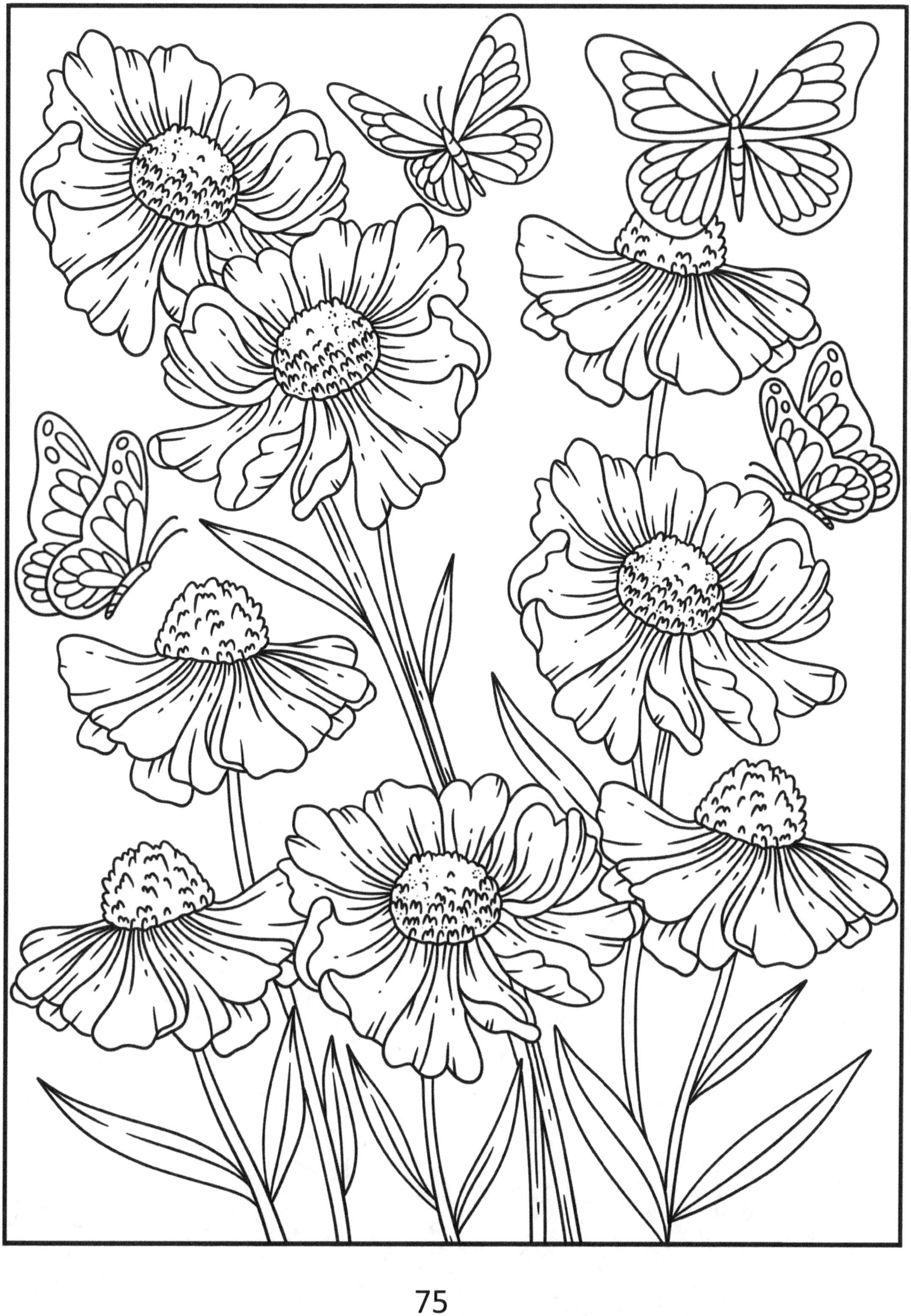

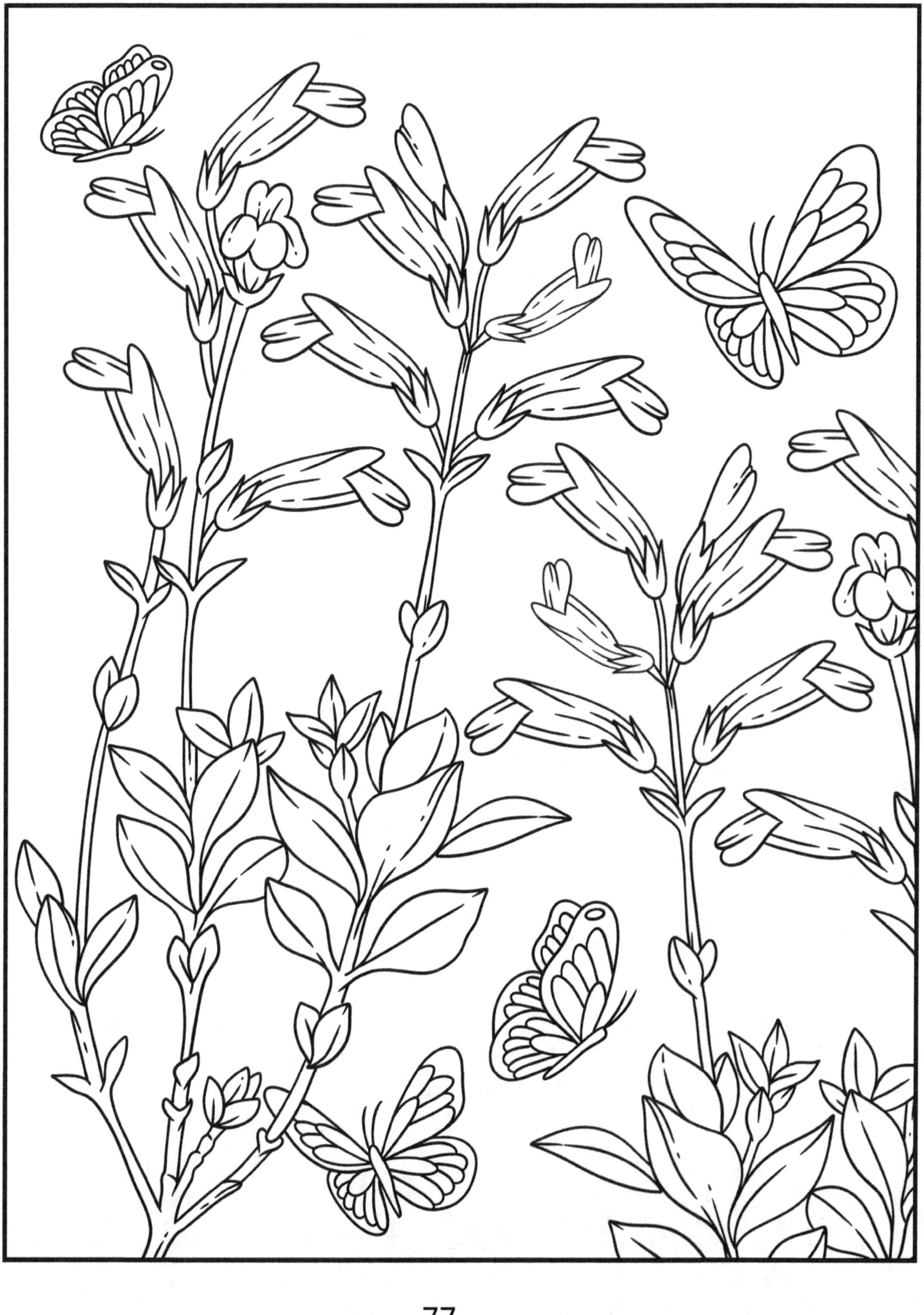

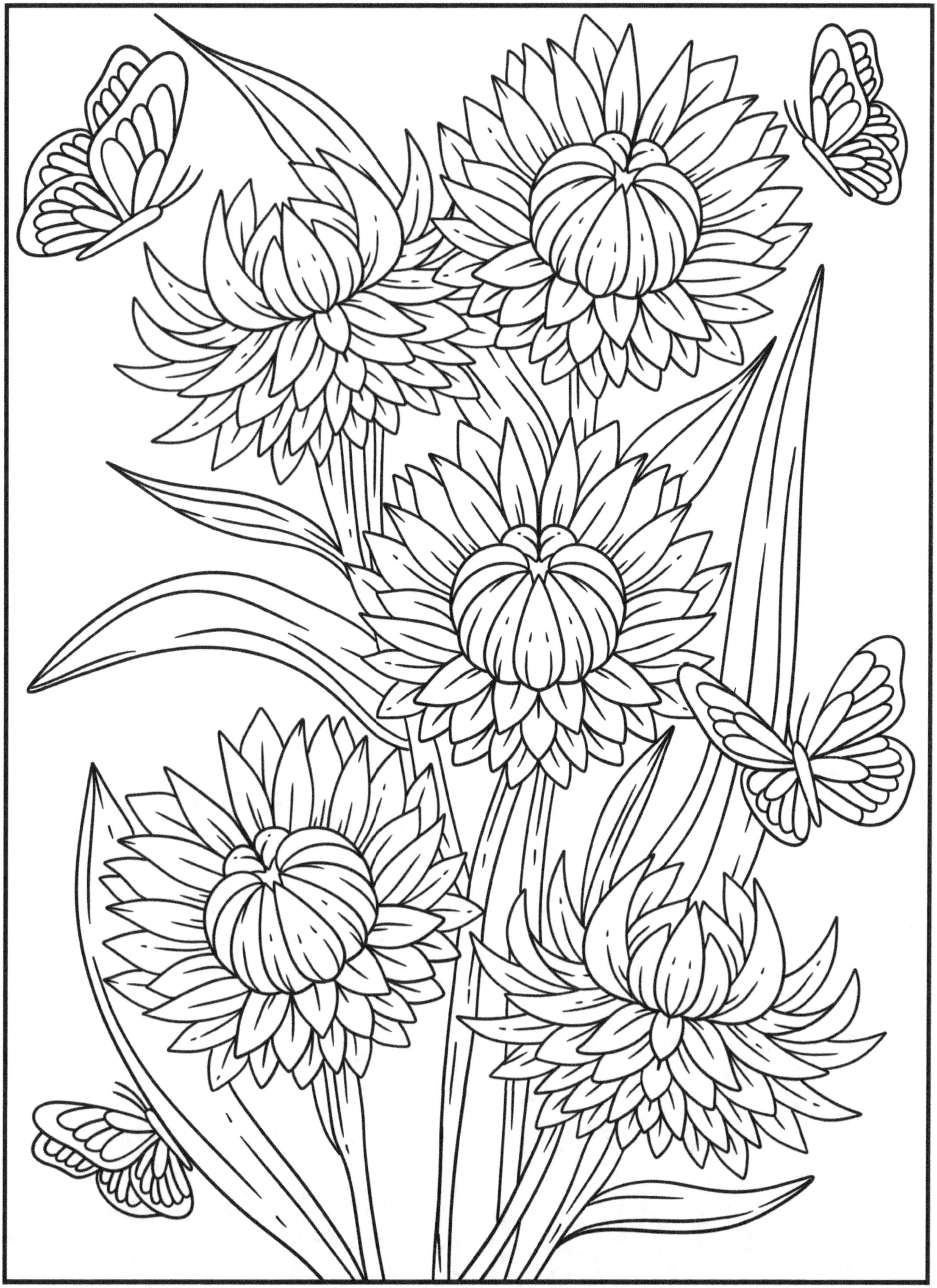

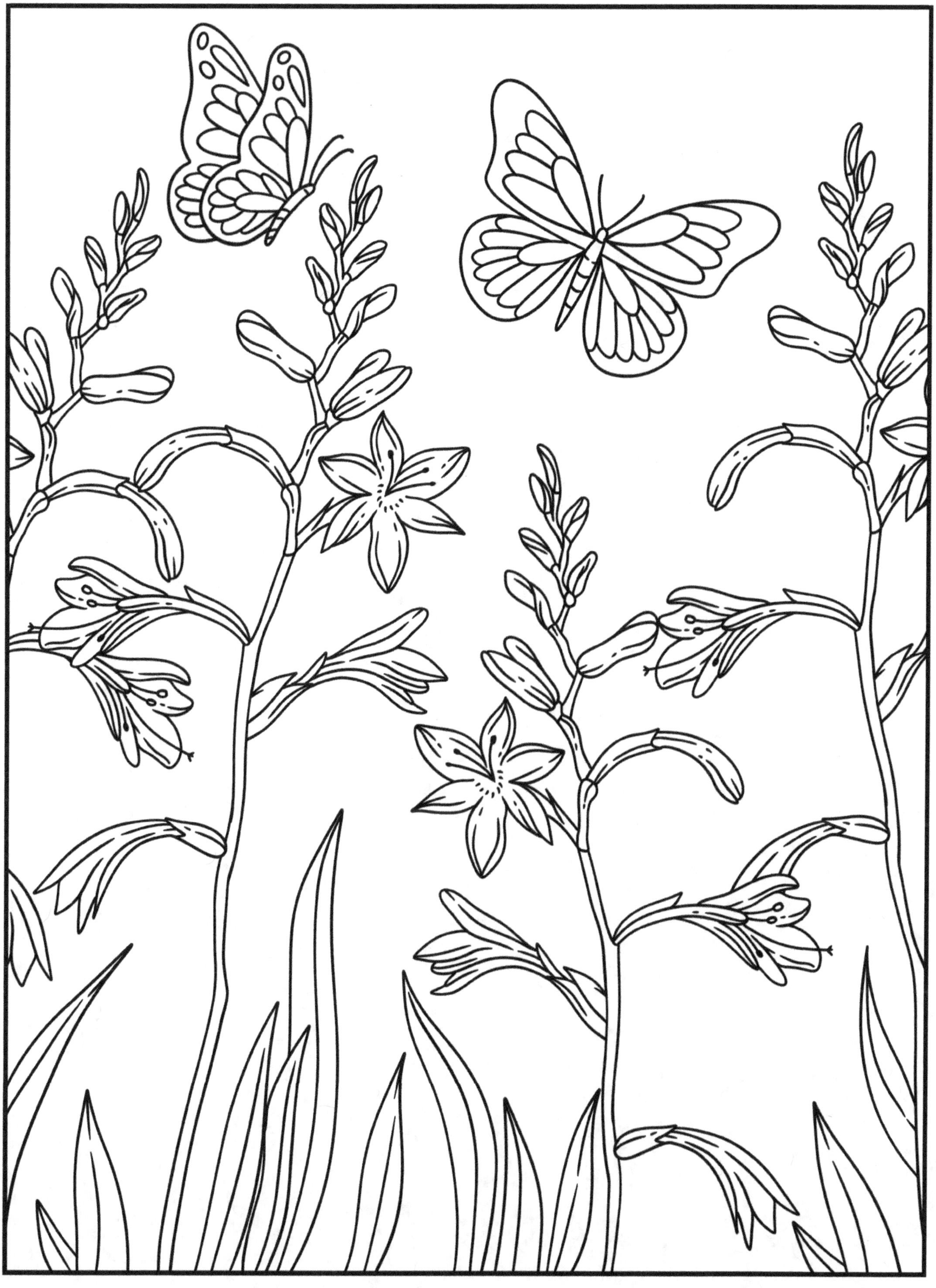

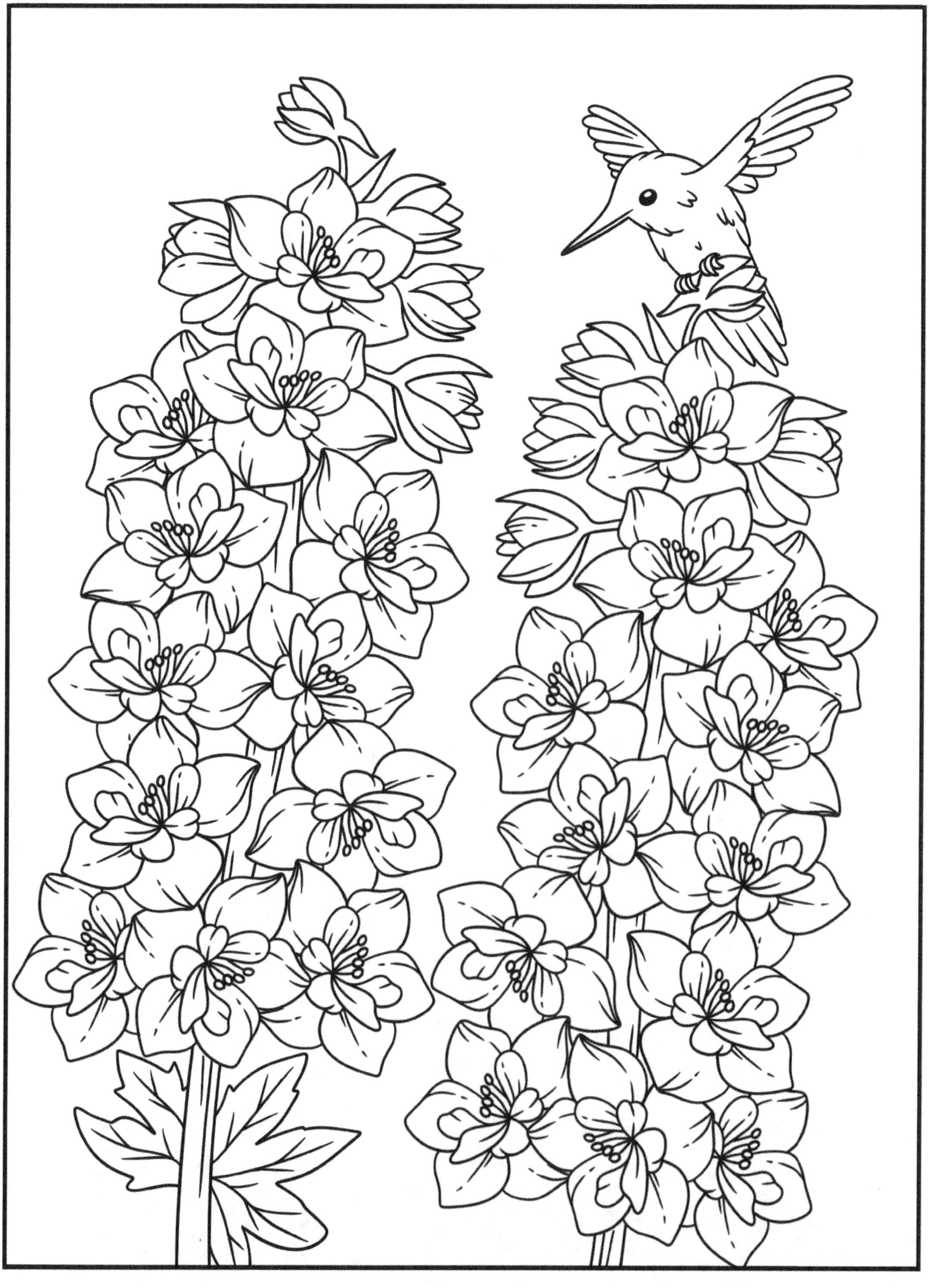

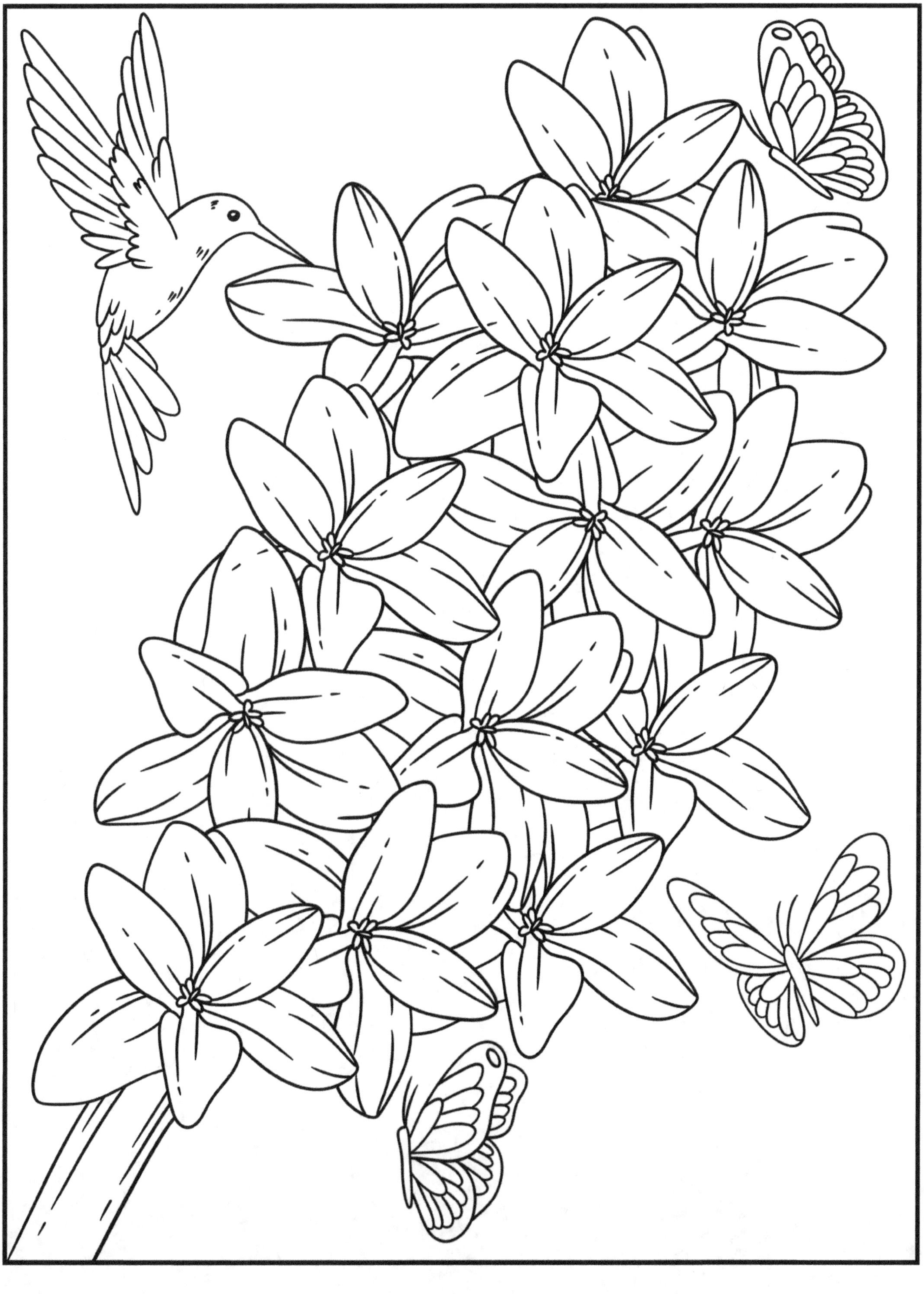

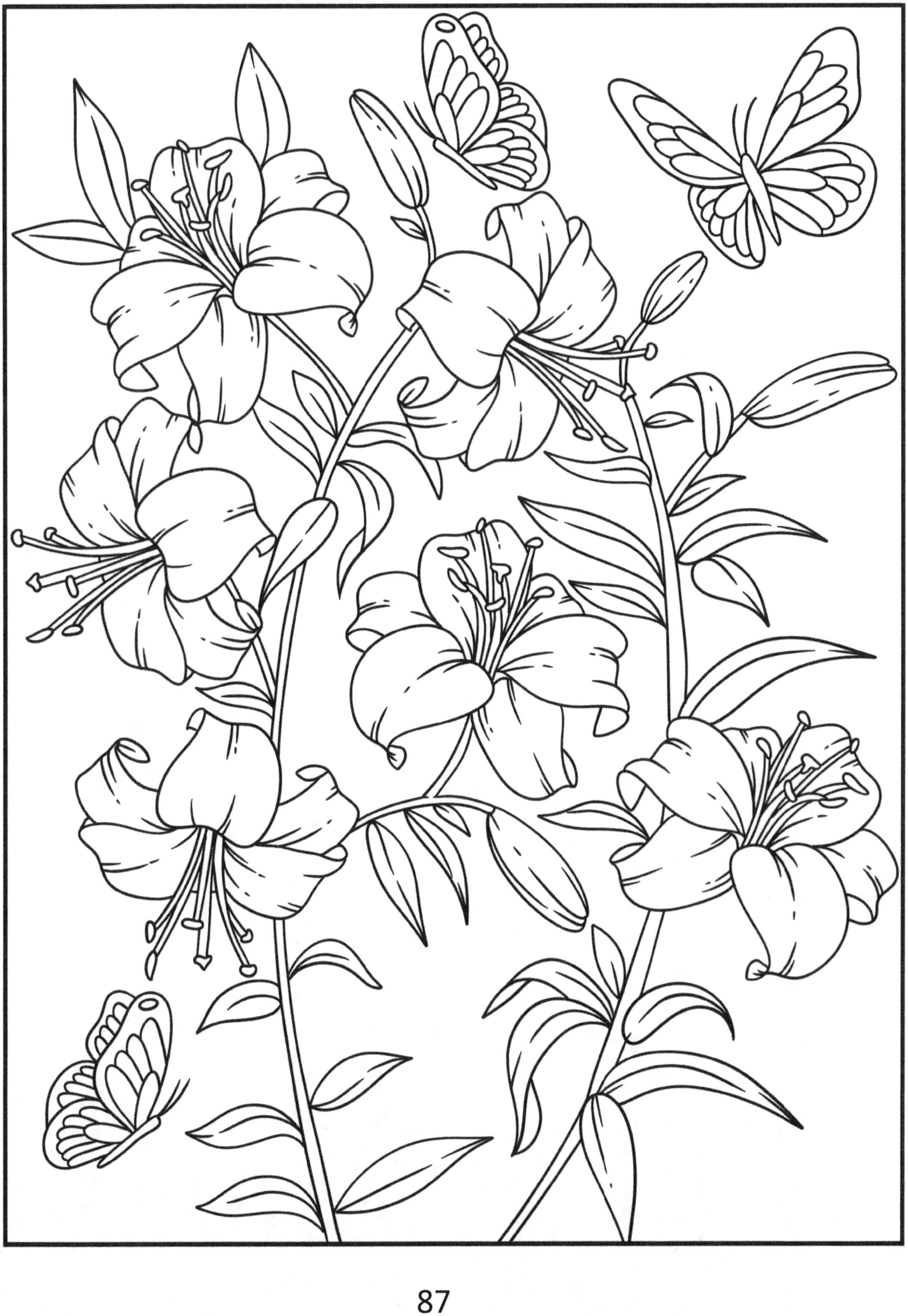

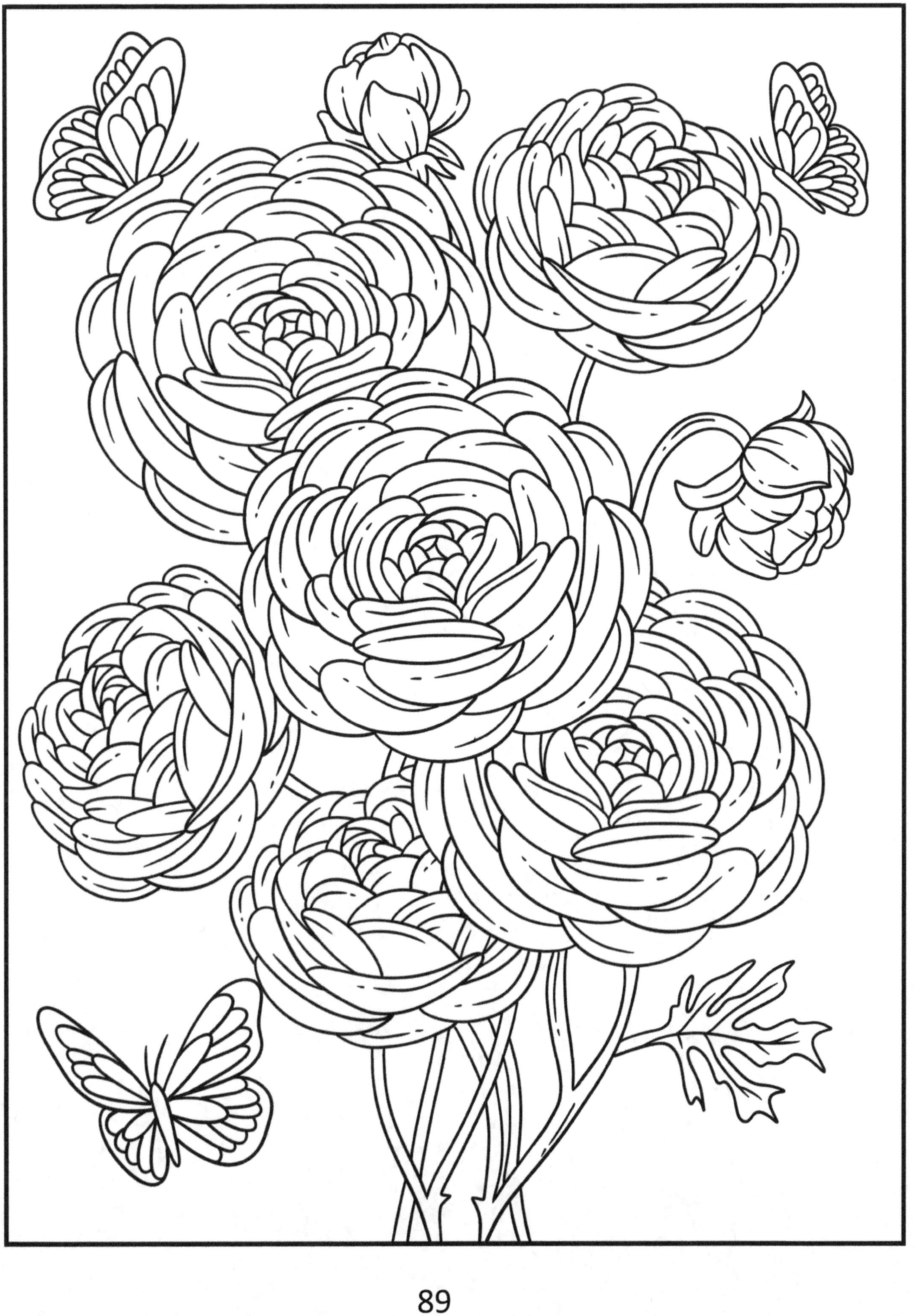

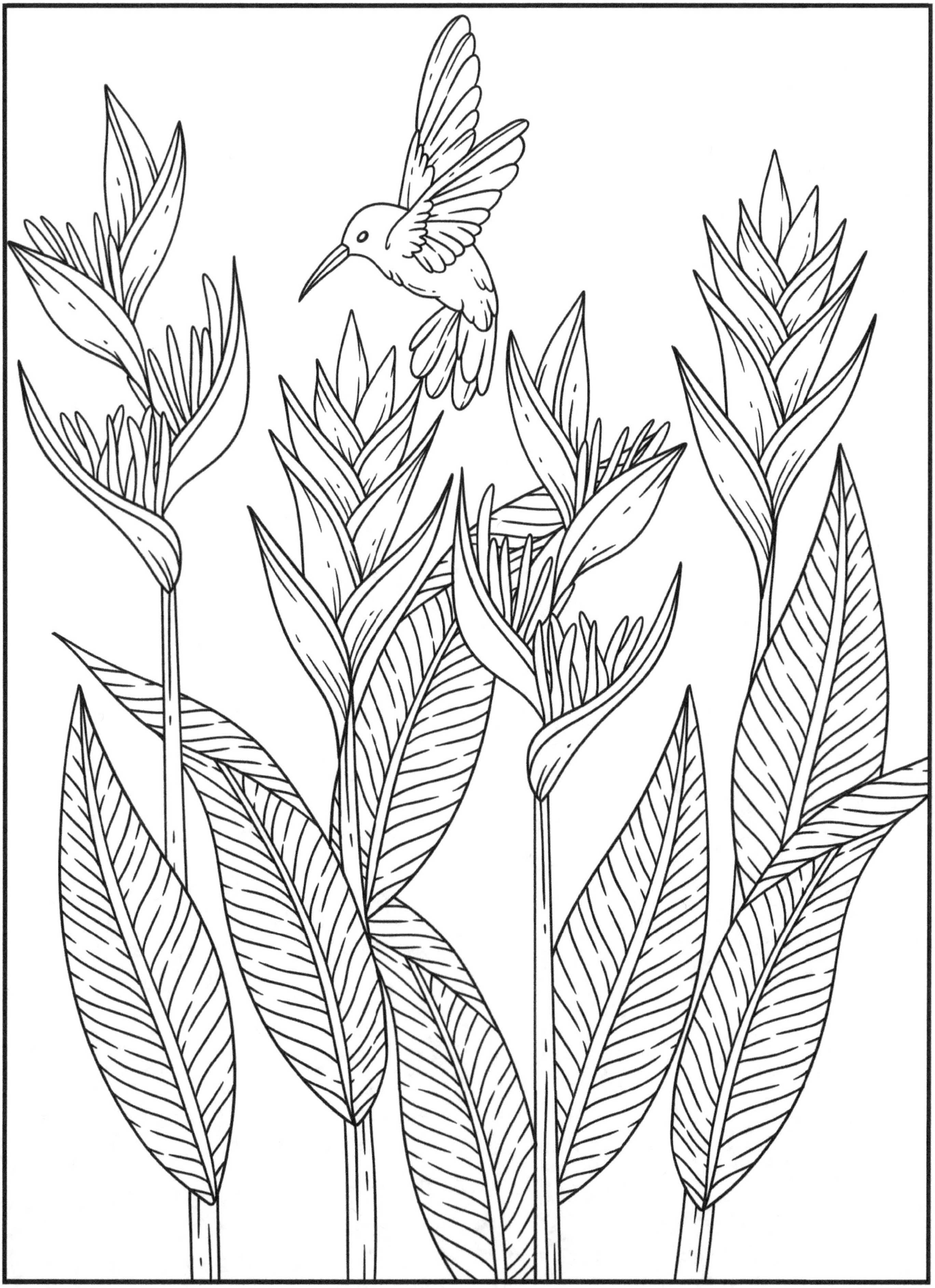

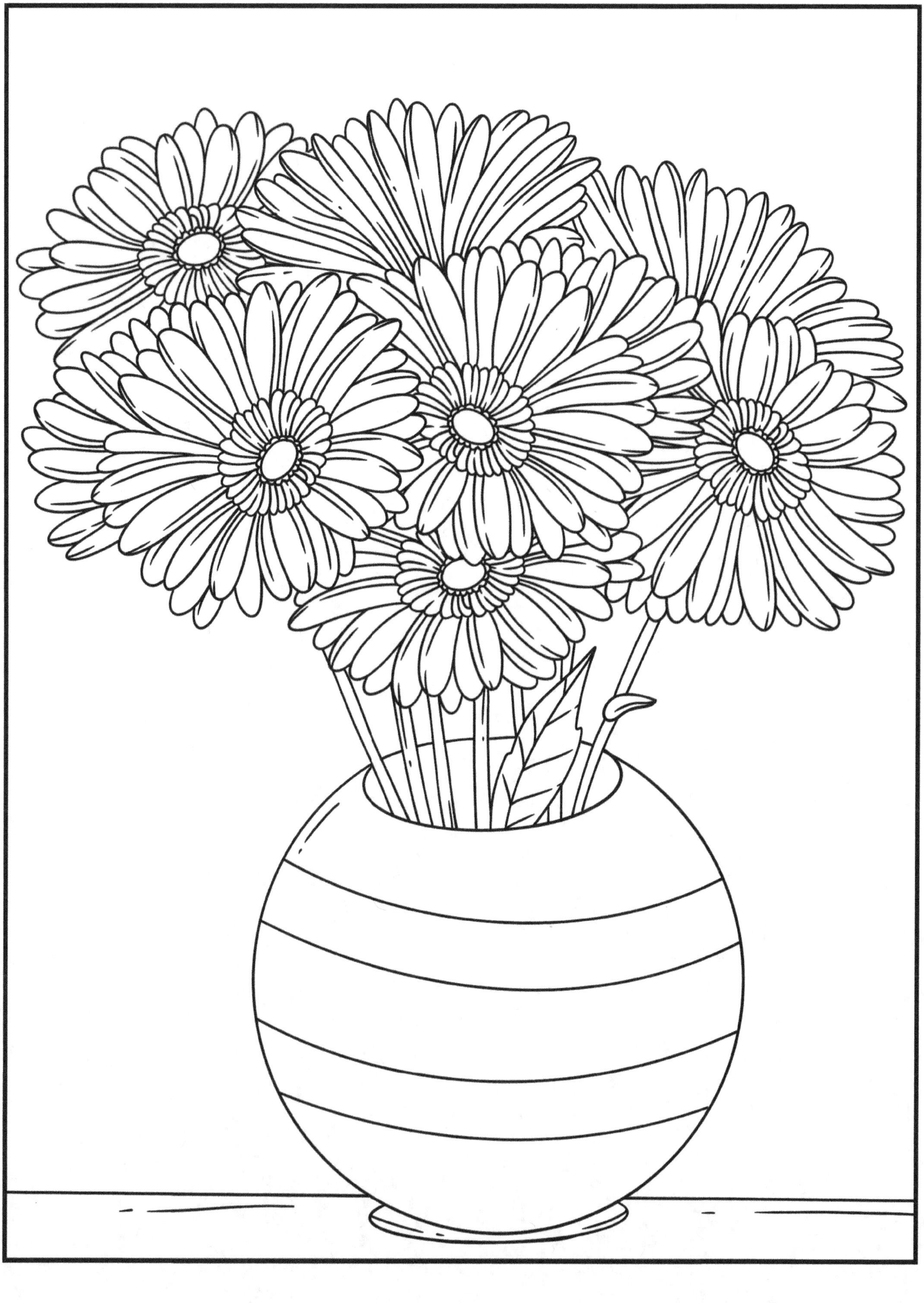

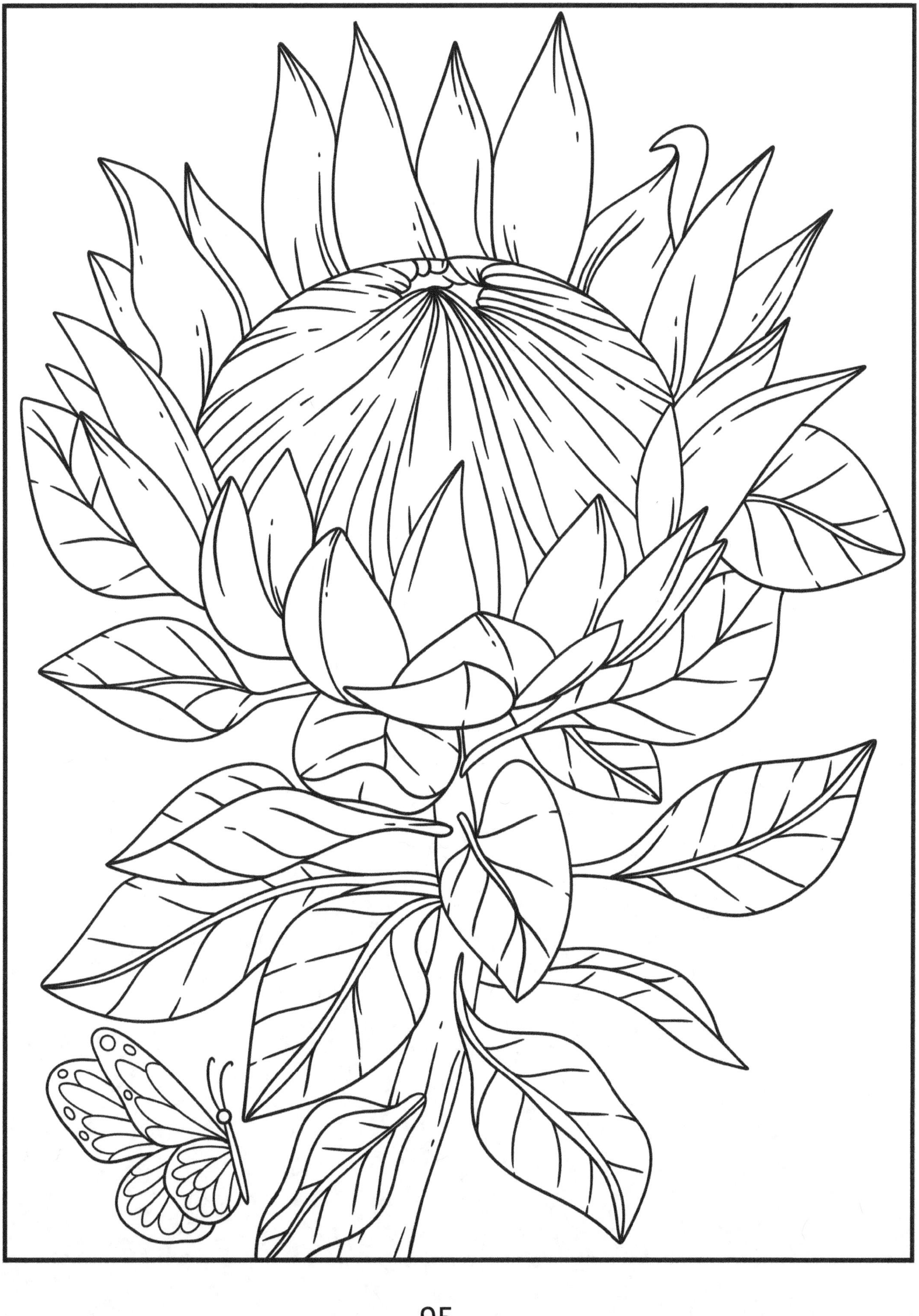

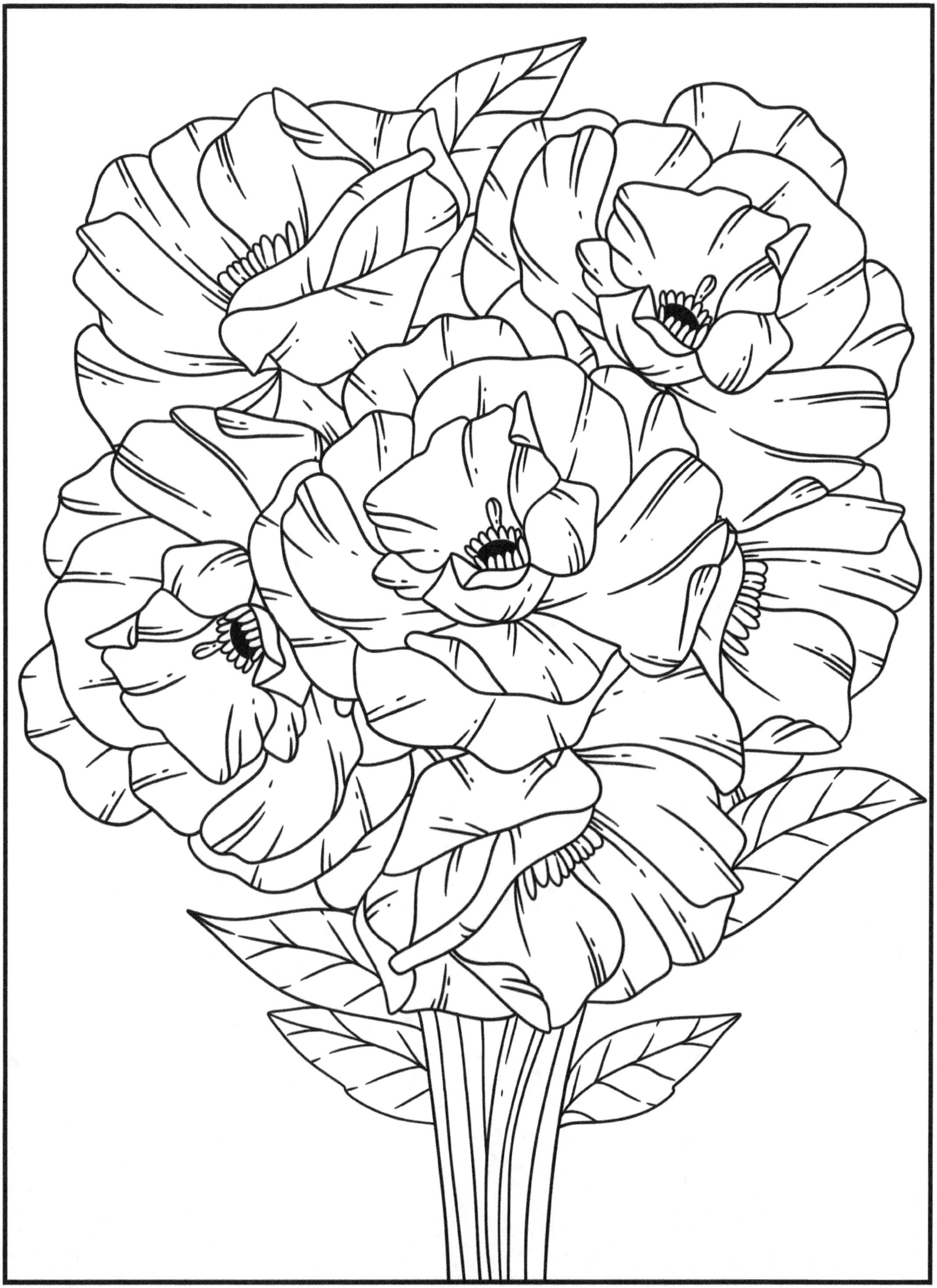

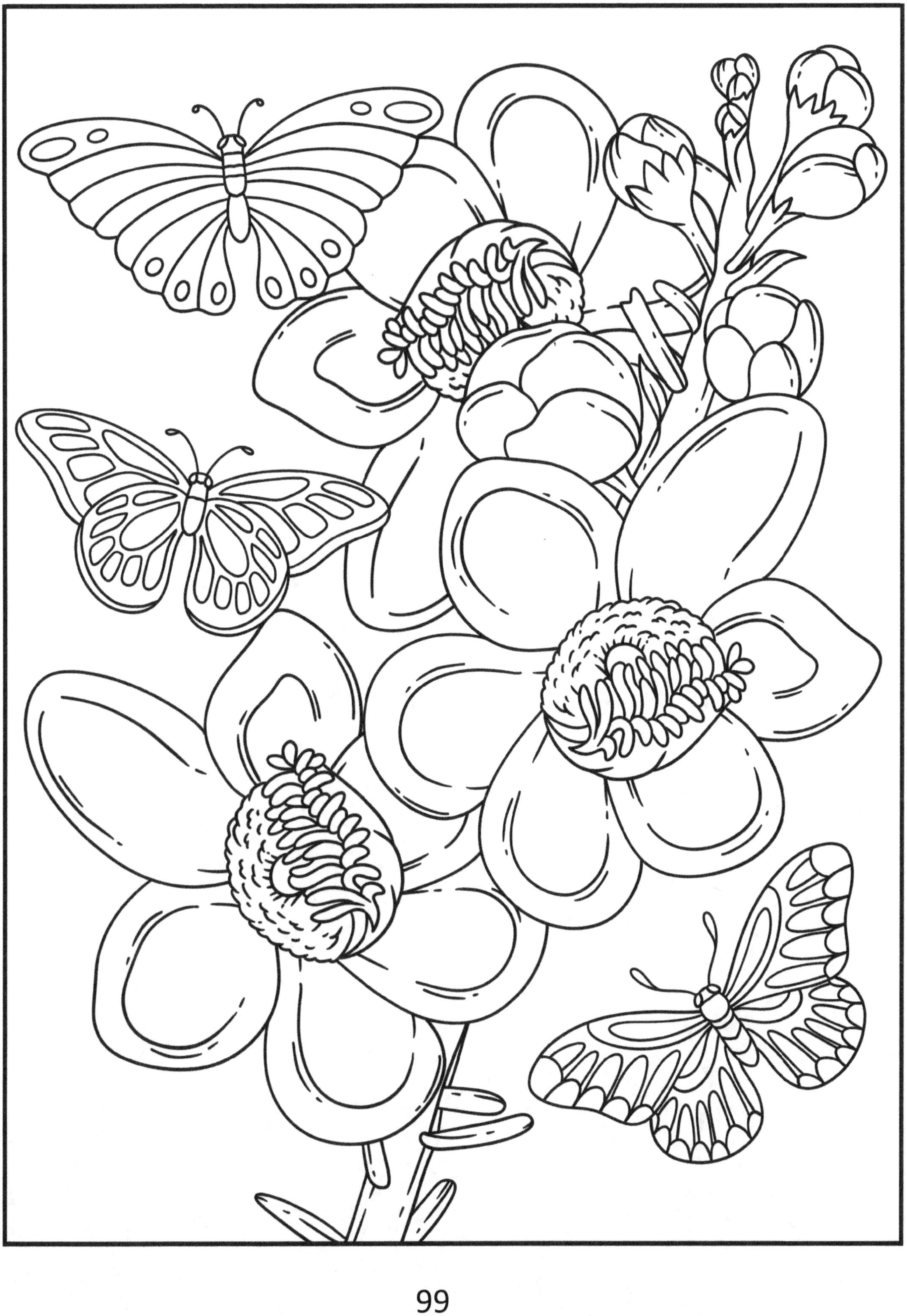

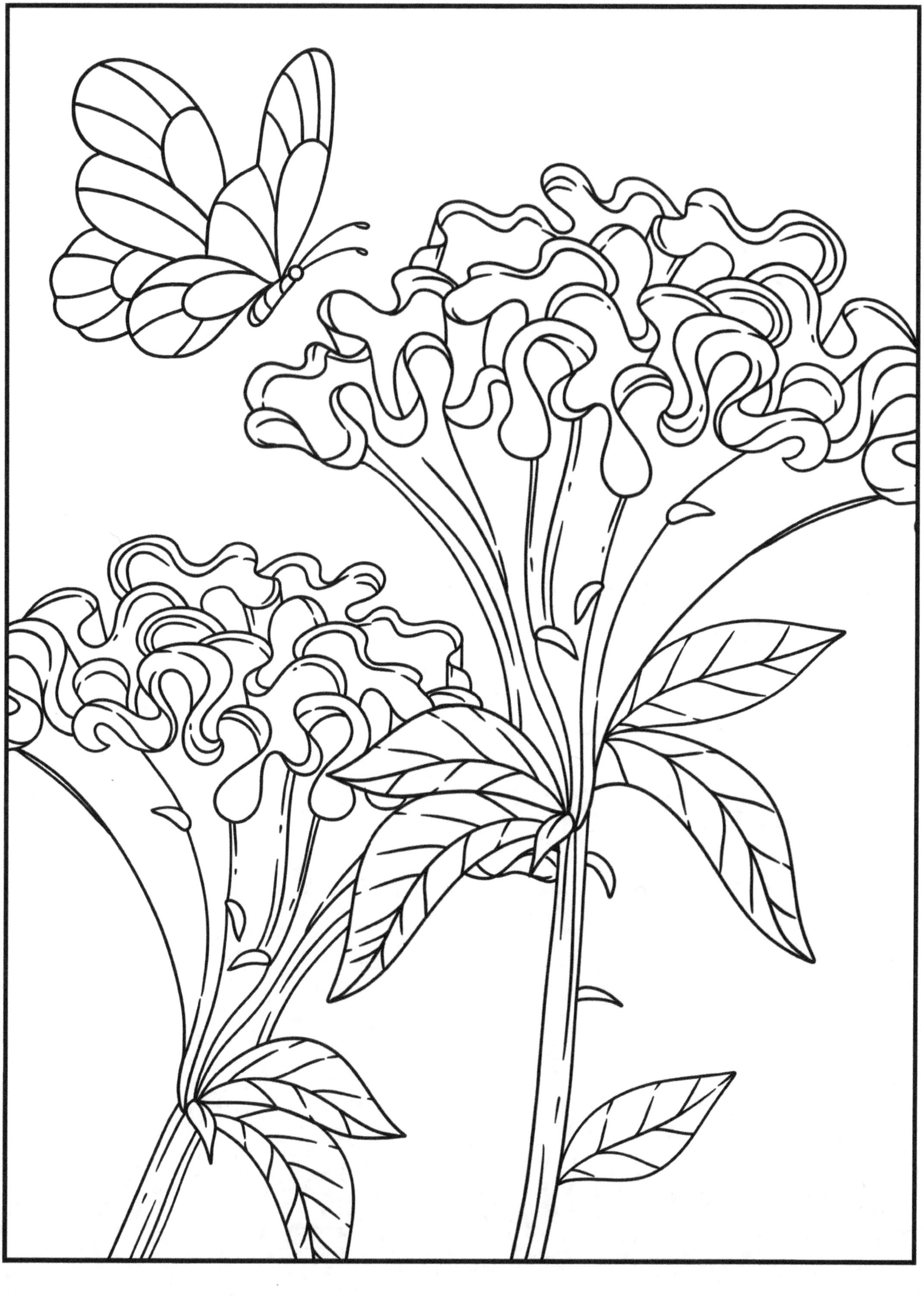

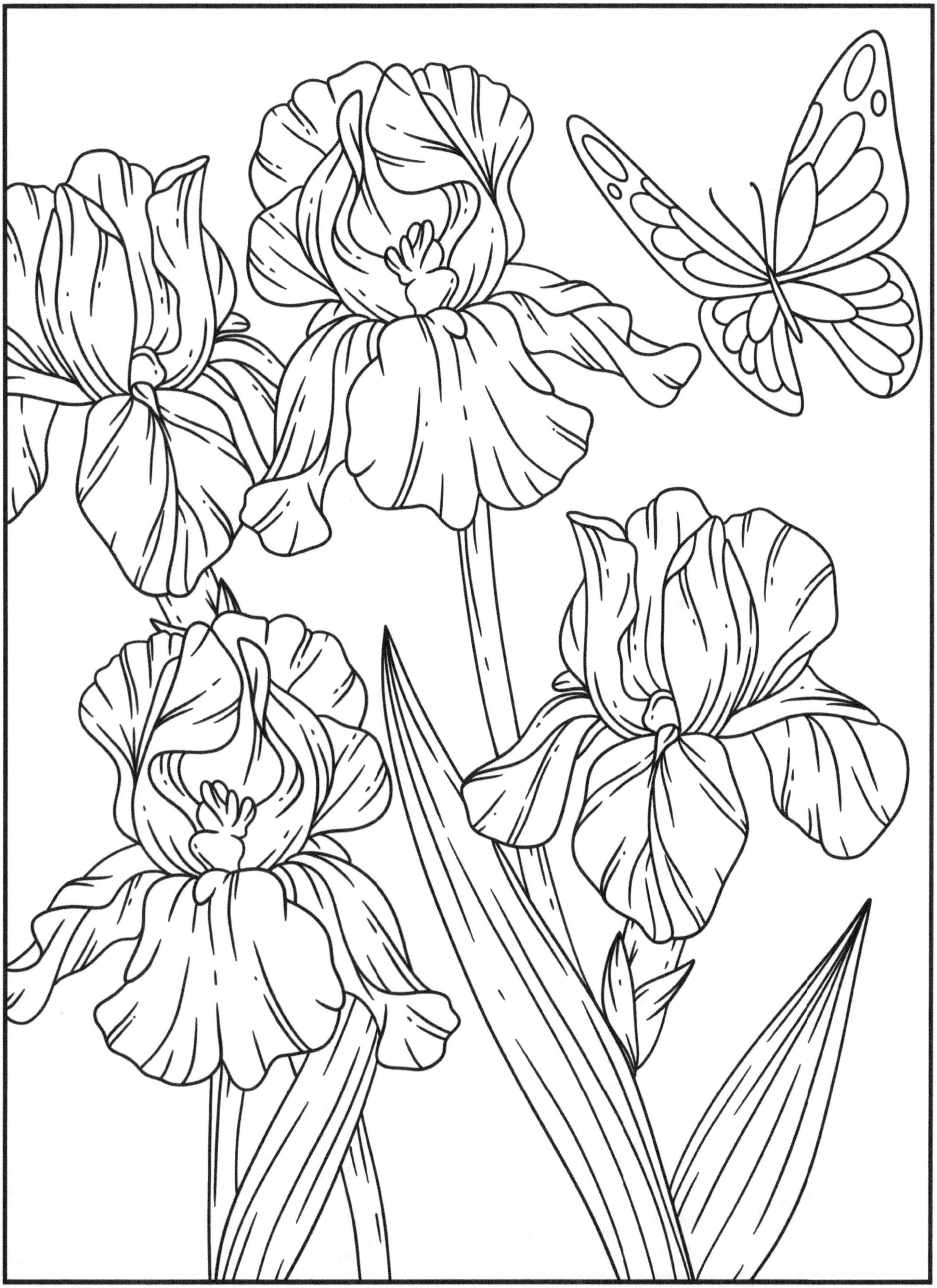

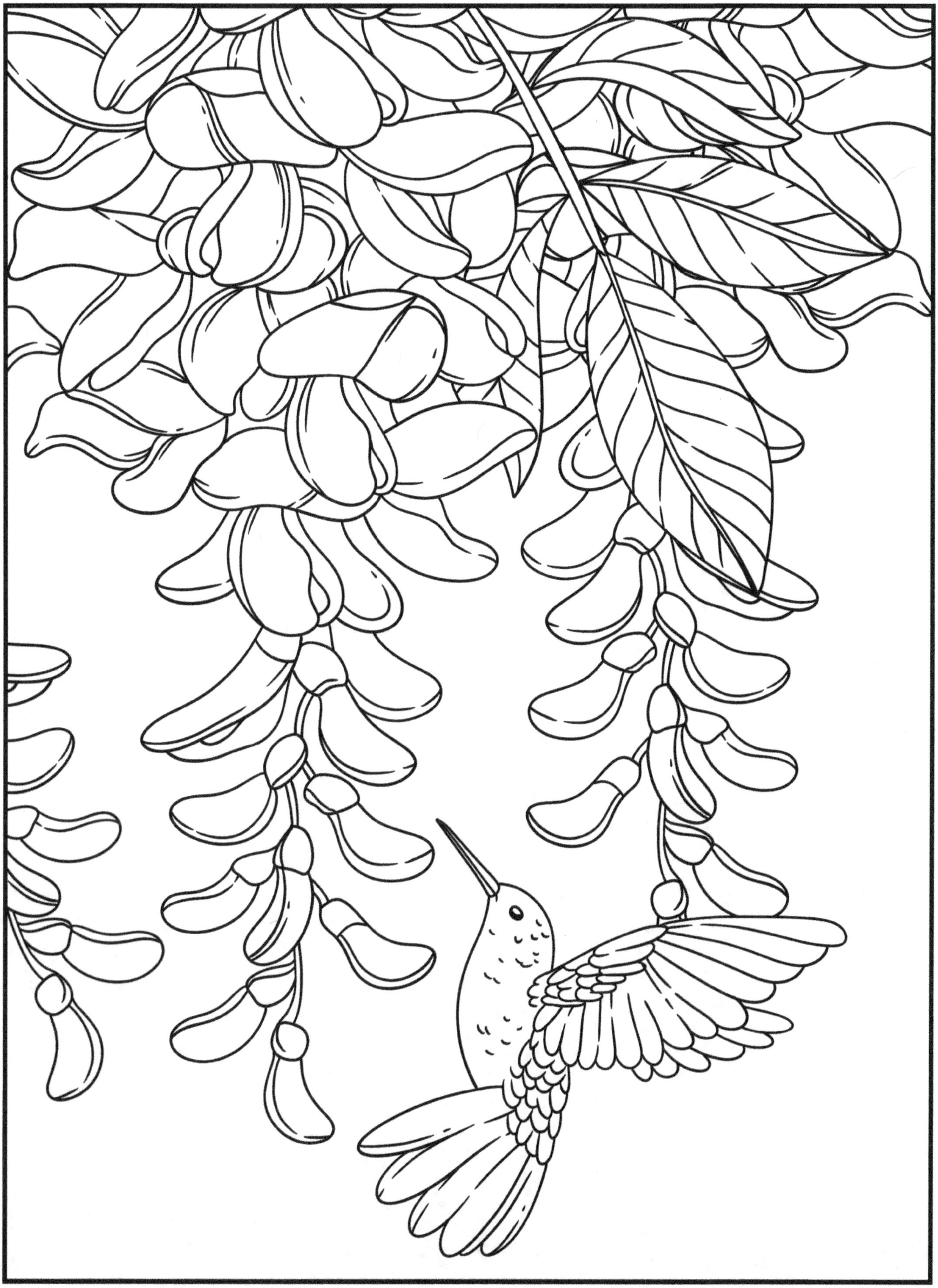

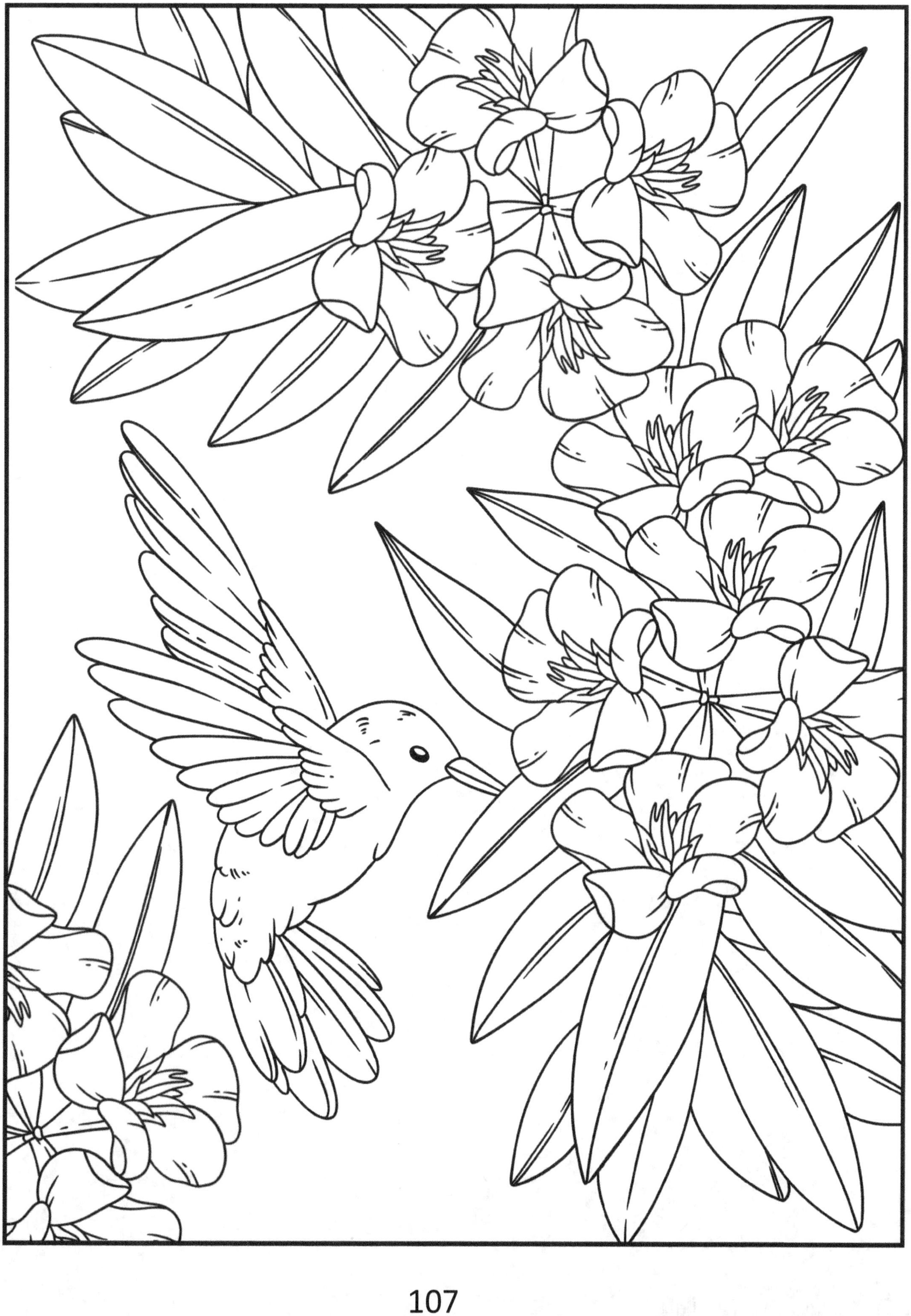

www.ingramcontent.com/pod-product-compliance
Lightning Source LLC
Chambersburg PA
CBHW080420290526
45791CB00008BA/2355
* 9 7 9 8 8 8 8 9 9 0 0 9 4 *